To wonderful guests
and great breakfasts
from Ogunquit, Maine.
Fondly,
Janet Glenn

Design by BookCreate
Seattle, Washington USA

ISBN: 978-0-692-86626-9

Printed in USA

Bentley patiently waiting for guests to arrive for breakfast

DEDICATED to Mana who taught me how to open my first can of chicken noodle soup, to play scrabble, and to make sure dinner always started with a salad and then included the four food groups; protein, starch, vegetable, and bread. How I wish you could see The Trellis House.

Thank you to my husband Glen Porter for trusting me when I said I wanted to leave my corporate career and open a Bed and Breakfast. Glen's response was, "how awesome that people are going to experience your cooking!" I am also so grateful that he subsequently left his career to join me in this wonderful adventure. Glen's kindness and connection to our guests and his willingness to do whatever is needed is valued beyond measure.

Thank you to my mother Martha whose love and support means everything to me. I get my love for creating an amazing environment and my perfectionist personality directly from that apple tree. She is still the first person that I call when something wonderful happens in my life.

To my father, Nathaniel who loves and collects cookbooks. I cannot think of a single thing I have ever done to displease him.

Thank you, Marcia Shannon, for editing my writing and recipe continuity and instructions. Special thanks to Sarah Santos for helping me develop and test recipes and to Jenn Hawley who encouraged me to do the hard work required to create this cookbook.

Finally, thank you Trellis House guests for your constant encouragement. Each time I was asked, "do you share your recipes?" I happily made a copy and shared. Now you can find them all in one place!

TABLE OF CONTENTS

Custard Filled Cornbread   58

Maple Nut Muffins   59

FIRST COURSES AND STARTERS   63

Homemade Granola Parfait with
Honey Crème and Fresh Fruit   66

Baked Apple Cranberry Oatmeal Brûlée   69

Grapefruit Brûlée with Vanilla Crème   70

Fresh Fruit with Vanilla Dip   71

Blueberry Banana Overnight Oatmeal   72

Fruit Salad with Champagne Mint Syrup   73

Strawberries Filled with Vanilla Mascarpone   74

Watermelon with Vanilla Crème and Grahams   75

Berry Granola Crème Brûlée   76

PANCAKES, FRENCH TOAST & WAFFLES   78

Almond Croissant French Toast
with Almond Praline Crunch   82

Bananas Foster French Toast
with Whipped Cream Cheese   84

Ham and Swiss Croissant French Toast
with Maple Dijon Syrup   86

Pecan Crunch Waffles with Molasses Butter   88

Brûléed Orange Challah French Toast   90

Pineapple Upside Down Pancakes
with Pineapple Maple Syrup   92

EGG DISH FAVORITES   106

Breakfast Strata with Sausage, Mushrooms,
and Monterey Jack   136

Breakfast Strata with Potatoes, Rosemary
and Fontina   138

Breakfast Bake   142

Sausage and Cheese Egg Pouf   144

HAPPY HOUR

Bruschetta with Red and Yellow Peppers,
Tomatoes, and Basil   150

Lobster or Shrimp Salad Rolls   152

Cuisinart Pizza Dough   153

Savory Pinwheels   154

Knorr Spinach Dip   156

Lemon Feta Pepper Dip   157

Perfect Picnic Deviled Eggs   158

Roasted Shrimp with Cocktail Sauce   160

Spinach and Cheese Custard Squares   161

Tzatziki Cucumber Garlic Dip   162

Whipped Feta and Red Pepper Dip   163

Zucchini And Tomato Tart   164

SIDES   168

Funeral Potatoes   172

Orange Glazed Sausages   173

Rosemary Home Fries with Roasted Tomato Aioli   174

TURNDOWN FAVORITES 181

COOKING SCHOOL 201

INTRODUCTION

If you are holding this cookbook you have most likely been our guest at The Trellis House. If not, we hope you will visit us soon. From the very first day we opened our doors we have been touched and overwhelmed by our guests' kindness and praise for our breakfasts. We come to this experience with no formal training preparing meals for guests. What guides us is a passion for food and serving our friends. With all the responsibilities associated with ensuring you have a great stay, the most enjoyable and satisfying aspect of owning and running a Bed and Breakfast is making sure that your breakfasts are unique, beautiful, and of course, delicious. As I often say, there are two things that we can't screw up...one is your Bed, and the other is your Breakfast.

Years before Glen and I ever thought of opening a Bed and Breakfast I began collecting recipes. Through my twenties, I read every food magazine I could get my hands on and continued this "hobby" throughout my corporate career, our lives in California, Boston, and finally Maine. I would tear recipes out from magazines in waiting rooms at the doctor's office (yes that was me), copy them from books, print them from the internet, and wrote down and developed my own recipes too. I had amassed boxes and boxes of recipes but never really looked at them after they went into those boxes. I often asked myself, "Why am I engaging in this somewhat obsessive, ongoing, twenty something year activity?" But I had no answer, other than I thoroughly enjoyed thinking and reading about food. I also of course enjoyed cooking at home.

When I was a boy, if you had asked me what I wanted to do when I "grew up" I would say, "I am going to own a small luxury beach hotel". This didn't make me popular with other kids. I spent much of my childhood in the kitchen baking simple things like brownies and cookies and received some early cooking lessons from my beloved grandmother. When it came time to go to college I decided to get a degree in Hotel, Restaurant Management and then a business degree, all the while working at the Four Seasons Hotel in Beverly Hills to pay for my education. I loved the hotel business but wanted to broaden my horizons.

Being in Los Angeles I had many exciting paths to pursue. I landed an entry level job in customer service, which evolved into corporate training, and then human resources and talent acquisition and worked at The Walt Disney Company, Warner Bros, and a visual effects studio called Digital Domain where I staffed hundreds of feature films, commercials, and music videos, my first being the movie Titanic.

After 18 years in Los Angeles, where Glen and I met, we decided to move back east to be nearer our families. We settled in Boston and both got corporate jobs. We also bought a small vacation home in Ogunquit where we would spend many happy weekends. After 10 years back in New England and at the age of 47, I left my corporate job as Vice President of Global Talent Acquisition with the largest speech recognition technology company in the world. Some thought it was premature to leave but I had made up my mind that I wanted to run my own business.

So, we started looking at small businesses in Ogunquit, Maine. I was convinced that I wanted to live and work in this perfect little beach town. We saw a variety of opportunities including an ice cream shop, a laundromat, an antique shop, a restaurant, and even a car wash, but none of them felt right. I began to get discouraged wondering what was going to be next when I got a call from my realtor who told me that a B&B was coming up for sale.

I drove up to Maine and saw The Trellis House. It wasn't until then that all my past dreams and experiences came back to me. The next day I asked Glen to meet me in Ogunquit to see the B&B we were going to buy and boy did it need work! Following your dreams can be a scary thing and I will always be grateful that Glen believed that I would be successful no matter what I chose to do.

Had I only known those many years ago, I surely would have focused on collecting breakfast recipes instead of gravitating towards baking, appetizers, and entrees. Once we bought The Trellis House I went through my boxes and boxes of recipes and cookbooks (which took months) and realized that I literally had to start from the beginning because I had neglected to collect breakfast recipes. We now had to figure out how to cook a major meal for up to 20 people each morning! Talk about stressful.

Slowly I began to define what breakfast meant to me as a business owner and my recipe development began anew but it wasn't until we opened our doors that I began to cook, and cook, and cook. Through much trial and joy and with two seasons behind us I have put all the recipes that we currently use down on paper. Some are "borrowed" and many are original but all are meant to convey what a homemade breakfast in Maine means to us.

Our menus always consist of two courses, sometimes more. We usually start breakfast with a just-baked pastry, alternatively a fruit course or other starter such as Brûléed Oatmeal or Homemade Granola Parfait. We try to organize our menus so that all the components work well together and make every effort to ensure that our guests never ever have a repeat dish during their stay. Our main courses vary and consequently we have organized our cookbook in sections as follows: Breakfast Baked Goods, Fruit Courses and Starters, Pancakes and Waffles, Egg Dish Favorites, and Sides.

Additionally, The Trellis House offers a "Happy Hour" in the late afternoon so our guests can enjoy some togetherness on our beautiful screened-in porch after the beach as well as a "surprise" turndown treat before bed. We have included a section for our favorite recipes for these activities as well.

Finally, we try to include our guests in our love for cooking by offering cooking classes held each month. A final section, Cooking Class Recipes, is also provided.

We hope you will enjoy memories of your stay with us by recreating some of our meals and treats at home. Thank you for inspiring us and allowing us the wonderful experience of being your hosts.

Sincerely,

Laurence and Glen

BREAKFAST
BAKED
GOODS

It is our goal at The Trellis House

to bake fresh and wonderful treats

each morning.

A B&B is a unique business because

it is clear to our visitors that

this is also our home.

Our guests are so appreciative

and surprised when we turn out

professional quality baked goods

for them to enjoy.

We are constantly amazed

at how people respond to our efforts.

THE
TRELLIS HOUSE
— · —
BREAKFAST BAKED GOODS

Signature Golden Banana Bread

Cheesy Onion Rolls

Raspberry Infused Corn Muffins

Cinnamon Raisin Oatmeal Scones
with Maple Drizzle

Honey Oatmeal Bread

Coconut Pineapple Muffins with Pineapple Butter

Blueberry Bread with Blueberry Butter

Cheddar Herb Biscuits

Raspberry Lemon Muffins with Raspberry Butter

Cranberry Pecan Muffins with Orange Butter

Oatmeal Streusel Muffins

THE
TRELLIS HOUSE

BREAKFAST BAKED GOODS

Lemon Ricotta Fritters

English Muffin Bread

Signature Coffee Cake

Popovers with Honey Butter

Blueberry Coffee Cake Muffins
with Cinnamon Butter

Peach Streusel Cake

Cranberry Bread
with Cranberry Butter

Make Ahead Streusel Mix

Monster Cinnamon Buns

Custard Filled Cornbread

Maple Nut Muffins

Signature Golden Banana Bread

2 Loaves

This recipe comes from Sarah Santos, my dear friend. Sarah is an excellent baker in her own right. She has been making this recipe for years and was kind enough to allow The Trellis House to adopt this perfect starter. We take this over the top by grilling each slice with honey and butter and dusting with confectioners' sugar.

11 ripe bananas (yes 11!)
1 1/2 cups brown sugar
2 sticks butter
1 tablespoon vanilla
3 eggs lightly beaten
1 teaspoon salt
2 teaspoons baking soda
4 cups flour

Place 6 bananas in their skins on a shallow baking pan and place in oven. Turn oven to 350° and bake for the duration of the pre-heat plus 10-15 minutes until the banana skins turn black.

Meanwhile, sift together flour, salt, and baking soda and set aside. In an electric stand mixer using the whisk attachment, mix 3 ripe bananas, brown sugar, vanilla, and butter until

well blended but lumpy. Remove hot bananas from their skins and add and mix until almost smooth. Make sure banana mixture cools slightly before stirring in the beaten eggs. Slice up the remaining 2 bananas and add to wet mixture. Fold together wet and dry mixtures.

Divide batter into 2 buttered loaf pans. Bake for 50-60 minutes until toothpick inserted in center comes out clean. Do not under bake. The tops will be a deep golden brown. Let cool in the pan and then transfer loaves to a wire rack to cool.

Cut into one inch slices. Heat griddle, melt butter, and grill the first side until golden. Drizzle with honey and grill the second side until golden. Dust with confectioners' sugar and garnish with berries.

Cheesy Onion Rolls

24 Rolls

These savory treats are truly wonderful. As you slowly unwind the delicate, flakey pinwheel of this roll, the cheese and onion is revealed. Plus, it's wicked good.

2 envelopes active dry yeast
1/2 cup warm water
1/2 cup sugar
1 cup milk warmed in microwave for 30 seconds
1/2 cup room temperature butter
1 1/2 teaspoons salt
2 large eggs
5 1/2 to 6 cups bread flour
2 cups shredded Colby or jack cheese
1/2 cup finely minced onion
1/4 cup dried chives
1 1/2 teaspoons garlic powder
4 tablespoons Hellman's mayonnaise

Combine yeast and warm water in the large bowl of a stand mixer. Let stand 5 minutes to soften yeast. Add sugar, milk, butter, salt, eggs, and 3 cups flour. Beat for 3 minutes until smooth; gradually add remaining flour until a soft dough is formed. Turn out onto lightly floured surface and knead 6-8 minutes, or until dough is smooth and elastic.

Place dough in lightly buttered bowl, turning once to coat. Let rise in a warm, draft free place for 1 hour or until doubled in size. Punch down and turn dough out onto a lightly floured surface and knead a few times. Let rest about 5 minutes.

Combine cheese, onions, chives, and garlic powder in a small bowl. Divide dough in half and roll each part out to a 15 x 12-inch rectangle. Spread each rectangle with 2 tablespoons mayonnaise and sprinkle with half of cheese mixture. Roll, starting at long side, and seal edges. Slice each roll into 12 slices and place cut side up on two well-greased 13 x 9-inch baking pans (2 rows of 6 = 12 rolls per pan). Cover and let rise 45-60 minutes, until doubled in size.

Bake in preheated 375° oven for 25-30 minutes, or until golden. Cool in pan 10 minutes. Serve warm with butter.

Raspberry Infused Corn Muffins

12 Muffins

This recipe comes from The Barefoot Contessa. Though easy to make, these muffins, infused with a center of raspberry jam are a show stopper.

3 cups all-purpose flour
1 cup sugar
1 cup medium cornmeal
2 tablespoons baking powder
1 1/2 teaspoons kosher salt
1 1/2 cups whole milk
1/2-pound unsalted butter melted and cooled
2 large eggs
3/4 cup good raspberry preserves

Preheat the oven to 350°. Spray lightly with non-stick spray and then line 12 large muffin cups with paper liners. In the bowl of an electric stand mixer fitted with a paddle attachment, mix the flour, sugar, cornmeal, baking powder, and salt. In a separate bowl, combine the milk, melted butter, and eggs. With the mixer on the lowest speed, pour the wet ingredients into the dry ones and stir until they are just blended. Spoon the batter into the paper liners, filling each one to the top. Bake for 30 minutes, until the tops are crisp and a toothpick comes out clean. Cool slightly and remove from the pan.

After the muffins cool, spoon the raspberry preserves into a pastry bag fitted with a large round tip. Push the tip of the bag through the top of the muffin and squeeze approximately 1 tablespoon of preserves into the middle. Repeat for each muffin. Dust with confectioners' sugar as I neglected to do for this photo.

Cinnamon Raisin Oatmeal Scones with Maple Drizzle

8 Scones

This recipe comes from Cook's Illustrated, one of my most treasured resources. This is no ordinary dry, biscuity scone. Moist and slightly cakey, this scone is cinnamony and slightly sweet and the graininess of the oats gives it an unbeatable texture.

1 1/2 cups old fashioned rolled oats
1/4 cup whole milk
1/2 cup heavy cream
1 large egg
1 1/2 cups unbleached all-purpose flour
1/3 cup sugar
2 teaspoons baking powder
1/4 teaspoon cinnamon
1/2 teaspoon salt
10 tablespoons very cold unsalted butter
    cut into 1/2 inch cubes
1/2 cup raisins
1 tablespoon sugar for dusting

Preheat oven to 375°. Spread the oats evenly on a baking sheet and toast in the oven until fragrant and lightly browned, 7-9 minutes; cool on a wire rack. Increase the oven temperature to 450°. Line a second baking sheet with

parchment paper. When the oats have cooled, measure out 2 tablespoons (for dusting the work surface and the dough) and set aside.

Whisk the milk, cream, and egg in a large measuring cup until incorporated; remove 1 tablespoon to a small bowl and reserve for glazing.

Pulse the flour, 1/3 cup sugar, baking powder, cinnamon, and salt in a food processor until combined, about four 1-second pulses. Scatter the cold butter evenly over the dry ingredients and pulse until the mixture resembles coarse cornmeal, about twelve 1-second pulses. Transfer the mixture to a medium bowl; stir in the cooled oats and raisins. Using a rubber spatula, fold in the liquid ingredients until large clumps form. Mix the dough by hand in the bowl until the dough forms a cohesive mass.

Dust the work surface with half of the reserved oats, turn the dough out onto the work surface, and dust the top with the remaining oats. Gently pat into a 7-inch circle about 1 inch thick. Cut the dough into 8 wedges and set on the lined baking sheet, spacing them about 2 inches apart. Brush the surfaces with the reserved egg mixture and sprinkle with 1 tablespoon sugar. Bake until golden brown, 12-14 minutes; cool the scones on the baking sheet on a wire rack for 5 minutes, then remove them to a rack and cool to room temperature, about 30 minutes.

For the maple drizzle: Mix 2 - 3 tablespoons of maple syrup with 1 cup of confectioners' sugar with a fork until smooth. Add more syrup until it will drizzle.

"Best bed and breakfast in Maine!"

We had a family of 6 and a baby looking for a place to stay this past May and we were fortunate enough to find the Trellis House. This was the first stop on our trip around Maine and was by far our favorite place of the trip! The owners are so nice and accommodating and really make it feel like home. We had an amazing breakfast every morning and met some great people. All the rooms were so nice and clean! The place was so amazing but what really made it an unforgettable stay were the two owners and their dog :) We can't wait to come back to the Trellis house. Definitely stay here if you get the chance it will not disappoint!

Honey Oatmeal Bread

2 Loaves

This bread is soft, warm, and slightly sweet with a terrific texture from the oats. We adapted a recipe that was attributed to the Von Trapp Family Lodge in Stowe, Vermont. When I bake this bread I always serve Glen a piece toasted with butter and say, "Here you go Liesl, enjoy"! He still laughs every time.

1/2 stick (1/4 cup) unsalted butter softened
1/3 cup brown sugar firmly packed
1 3/4 cups old fashioned rolled oats
2 tablespoons honey
2 1/2 cups hot water
2 - envelopes active dry yeast
5 - 6 cups all-purpose flour
2 teaspoons salt
1 egg plus 1 tablespoon water beaten

In the large bowl of an electric stand mixer with a dough hook attached, combine butter, brown sugar, honey and 1 1/2 cups oats reserving 1/4 cup. Turn mixer on medium and blend in hot water for a minute or so and then let mixture stand until lukewarm. Sprinkle yeast over mixture and let stand until foamy, about 5 minutes.

With mixer on low stir in five cups of flour and salt, stirring until mixture forms a dough, then turn out onto a floured surface. Knead dough 10 minutes adding as much additional flour as needed to form an elastic and smooth dough. Let rest, covered with an inverted bowl for 15 minutes.

Lightly spray two loaf pans with oil. Form dough into two loaves, transfer to pans and brush tops with egg wash, sprinkling with remaining oats. Let rise until doubled in bulk, about 1 hour. Bake in middle of a 350° oven for 45-50 minutes until brown. Bottoms will sound hollow when tapped. Cool completely before making thick slices. Toast and generously butter right before serving.

Coconut Pineapple Muffins with Pineapple Butter

12 Muffins

You feel like you are on vacation when you bite into this moist and sunny muffin. We serve it with pineapple butter on the side and our guests just love it.

1 stick plus 1 tablespoon unsalted butter melted
2 cups all-purpose flour
2 teaspoons baking powder
3/4 teaspoon salt
1/2 teaspoon cinnamon
1 cup dark brown sugar packed
3/4 cup walnuts
2 large eggs
1/2 cup unsweetened flaked coconut
3/4 cup unsweetened crushed pineapple drained
1/2 cup fat free milk
1/2 cup unsweetened pineapple juice
1 teaspoon vanilla

Place oven rack in middle position and preheat oven to 350°. Lightly spray a 12-cup muffin tin with non-stick spray and place liners in each cup.

Whisk together flour, baking powder, salt, cinnamon,

and brown sugar until well combined. Pulse walnuts in a food processor until finely ground. Whisk eggs in a large bowl until combined well, then whisk in ground walnuts, coconut, pineapple, milk, pineapple juice, vanilla, and butter until combined well. Add flour mixture and stir with a wooden spoon until just combined.

Divide batter among muffin cups and bake until puffed and springy to the touch, 30-35 minutes. Remove muffins from cups and transfer to a rack to cool.

For the Pineapple Butter: Use a fork to mix 1 stick softened butter in a small bowl with 1 tablespoon crushed pineapple and 1 teaspoon brown sugar. Spoon into a ramekin, sprinkle with salt, and chill slightly until ready to serve.

Blueberry Bread with Blueberry Butter

1 Loaf

This bread is somewhere between bread and cake. It is moist and rustic and not too sweet. We have one baking practically around the clock and often welcome guests with a fresh slice to enjoy with their champagne or serve at breakfast with blueberry butter.

1 stick butter room temperature
1 1/2 cups sugar plus extra 2 tablespoons for sprinkling
1 cup sour cream
3 large eggs
3 cups all-purpose flour sifted
4 teaspoons baking powder
1 teaspoon salt
2 cups fresh Maine blueberries

Preheat oven to 350°. Butter and flour two loaf pans.

In a stand mixer using a paddle attachment mix butter, sugar, and sour cream until combined. Add eggs one at a time until blended. Sift flour, baking powder, and salt together and add until batter just comes together. Gently stir in blueberries. Spoon batter into pan and sprinkle top with extra sugar. Bake for 50-60 minutes until tester comes out clean. Transfer to a wire rack to cool. Serve warm with blueberry butter.

For the Blueberry Butter: Use a fork to mix 1 stick softened butter in a small bowl with 1 tablespoon blueberry preserves. Spoon into a ramekin, sprinkle with salt, and chill slightly until ready to serve.

Cheddar Herb Biscuits

6 Biscuits

These cheddar herb biscuits are perfect for our breakfast sandwiches with ham, chive scrambled eggs, and a slice of slow roasted tomato.

1 1/2 cups all-purpose flour
1 1/2 cups cake flour
1 tablespoon baking powder
1/2 teaspoon baking soda
1 teaspoon salt
8 tablespoons butter cut into 1/2 inch pieces
4 tablespoons vegetable shortening cut into 1/2 inch pieces
1 1/4 cups buttermilk
2 cups sharp cheddar cheese grated
1 tablespoon chopped fresh chives

Adjust oven rack to upper middle position and heat oven to 425°. Butter a 9-inch cake pan. Combine flours, baking powder, soda, and salt in a large bowl. Rub butter and shortening into flour mixture until it resembles coarse meal. Stir in buttermilk just until combined and then gently stir in cheddar and herbs.

Using 1/2 cup measure, scoop dough to make 6 heaping biscuits into prepared pan, placing 5 around the perimeter and 1 in the center and bake until puffed and golden, 20-25 minutes. Transfer to wire rack to cool.

"Wonderful experience"

My wife and I spend a delightful 2 nights at The Trellis House. Laurence goes out of his way to make sure we are comfortable, well fed and enjoying some quality time at the Inn. Laurence makes the best breakfast and serves it with a flare. Great location near the beach, relaxing surroundings at a good price.
We will be back!

Raspberry Lemon Muffins with Raspberry Butter

12 Muffins

My favorite things to bake are muffins and these are my favorite muffins to bake. The raspberries break down into the finished product to create little pockets of fruit which combine deliciously with the not too sweet, slightly tangy, and light texture of the cake. Trust.

3 cups all-purpose flour
1 cup sugar
1 tablespoon baking powder
1/2 teaspoon baking soda
1 1/2 cups plain yogurt
2 large eggs
8 tablespoons butter melted and cooled
2 cups fresh raspberries
1 teaspoon lemon zest
turbinado or regular sugar

Adjust oven rack to middle position and preheat oven to 375°. Lightly spray a 12-cup muffin tin with non-stick spray and place liners in each cup. Measure dry ingredients into a large bowl and fluff with a whisk. In a separate bowl whisk yogurt and eggs together until smooth. Gently fold into flour mixture just until barely combined. Fold in the melted butter but do not over mix. Stir in raspberries and lemon zest.

Using a large scoop, divide batter evenly among muffin cups filling each to the top. Sprinkle generously with sugar. Bake, rotating halfway through, until muffins are golden and a toothpick inserted in the center comes out clean, about 20-25 minutes. Let cool for about 10 minutes before serving.

For the Raspberry Butter: Use a fork to mix 1 stick softened butter in a small bowl with 1 tablespoon raspberry preserves. Spoon into a ramekin, sprinkle with salt, and chill slightly until ready to serve.

CRANBERRY PECAN MUFFINS WITH ORANGE BUTTER

9 Muffins

Correct folks, it's not always summer in Maine! Fall is the perfect time to expand our repertoire with cranberries and fall baked goods and this muffin is ideal.

Streusel Topping:
3 tablespoons all-purpose flour
4 teaspoons sugar
1 tablespoon packed brown sugar
2 tablespoons butter cut into 1/2 inch pieces softened
Pinch salt
1/2 cup pecan halves

Muffins:
1 1/3 cups all-purpose flour
1 1/2 teaspoons baking powder
1 teaspoon salt
1 1/4 cups pecans halves toasted and cooled
1 cup plus 1 tablespoon sugar
2 large eggs
6 tablespoons butter melted and cooled slightly
1/2 cup whole milk
2 cups fresh cranberries
1 tablespoon confectioners' sugar

Adjust oven rack to upper-middle position and heat oven to 425°.

For the streusel topping: Process flour, granulated sugar, brown sugar, butter, and salt in food processor until mixture resembles coarse sand, 4-5 pulses. Add pecans and process until pecans are coarsely chopped, about 4 pulses. Transfer to small bowl; set aside.

Spray 12-cup muffin tin with baking spray and place liners in each cup. Whisk flour, baking powder, 3/4 teaspoon salt together in bowl; set aside.

Process toasted pecans and granulated sugar until mixture resembles coarse sand, 10-15 seconds. Transfer to large bowl and whisk in eggs, butter, and milk until combined. Whisk flour mixture into egg mixture until just moistened and no streaks of flour remain. Set batter aside 30 minutes to thicken.

Pulse cranberries, remaining 1/4 teaspoon salt, and confectioners' sugar in food processor until very coarsely chopped, 4-5 pulses. Using rubber spatula, fold cranberries into batter. Use ice cream scoop to divide batter equally among prepared muffin cups, slightly mounding in middle. Evenly sprinkle streusel topping over muffins, gently pressing into batter to adhere. Bake until muffin tops are golden and just firm, 17-18 minutes, rotating muffin tin halfway through baking time. Transfer to a wire rack to cool.

For the Orange Butter: Use a fork to mix 1 stick of softened butter in a small bowl with 1 tablespoon orange marmalade. Spoon into a ramekin and chill slightly until ready to serve.

Oatmeal Streusel Muffins

12 Muffins

I love the texture and taste of oatmeal in baked goods. This is a Cook's Illustrated recipe that I think produces the most wonderful muffin. It is elegant, so flavorful, and a bit earthy.

Streusel:
1/2 cup old fashioned rolled oats
1/3 cup flour
1/3 cup pecans chopped fine
1/3 cup light brown sugar packed
1 1/4 teaspoons cinnamon
1/8 teaspoon salt
4 tablespoons melted butter

Muffins:
2 tablespoons unsalted butter
6 tablespoons unsalted butter melted
2 cups old fashioned rolled oats
1 3/4 cups flour
1 1/2 teaspoons salt
3/4 teaspoon baking powder
1/4 teaspoon baking soda
1 1/3 cups light brown sugar packed
1 3/4 cups whole milk
2 large eggs beaten

For the streusel: Combine oats, flour, pecans, light brown sugar, cinnamon, and salt in medium bowl. Drizzle melted butter over mixture and stir to thoroughly combine; set aside.

For the muffins: Lightly spray a 12-cup muffin tin with non-stick spray and place liners in each cup. Melt 2 tablespoons butter in 10-inch skillet over medium heat. Add oats and cook, stirring frequently, until oats turn golden brown and smell of cooking popcorn, 6-8 minutes. Transfer oats to food processor and process into fine meal, about 30 seconds. Add flour, salt, baking powder, and baking soda to oats and pulse until combined, about 3 pulses.

Stir 6 tablespoons melted butter and sugar together in large bowl until smooth. Add milk and eggs and whisk until smooth. Using whisk, gently fold half of oat mixture into wet ingredients, tapping whisk against side of bowl to release clumps. Add remaining oat mixture and continue to fold with whisk until no streaks of flour remain. Set aside batter for 20 minutes to thicken. Meanwhile, adjust oven rack to middle position and heat oven to 375°.

Using ice cream scoop or large spoon, divide batter equally among prepared muffin cups. Evenly sprinkle topping over muffins (about 2 tablespoons per muffin). Bake until toothpick inserted in center comes out clean, 18-25 minutes, rotating muffin tin halfway through baking.

Let muffins cool in muffin tin on wire rack for 10 minutes. Remove muffins from muffin tin and serve or let cool completely before serving.

Lemon Ricotta Fritters

Serves 4

Picture a small plate piled high with seven or eight little golden nuggets dusted with powdered sugar and drizzled with strawberry jam. Now dive into these mouthwatering delights.

3/4 cup all-purpose flour
2 teaspoons baking powder
1 teaspoon grated lemon zest
1/4 teaspoon salt
1 cup whole milk ricotta
2 large eggs
3 tablespoons sugar
1 1/2 teaspoons pure vanilla extract
confectioners' sugar
strawberry jam
canola oil for frying

Heat 2 inches of oil in a large, heavy saucepan until it reaches 370° on a deep fry thermometer.

Whisk together the flour, baking powder, zest, and salt in a bowl. Whisk together the ricotta, eggs, sugar, and vanilla in another bowl. Whisk the ricotta mixture into the flour mixture.

Working in batches, gently drop a tablespoon of batter at a time into the hot oil and fry, turning occasionally, until deep golden, about 3 minutes per batch. Transfer to paper towels to drain. Place on a plate and drizzle with jam. Dust generously with confectioners' sugar and serve with a bowl of extra strawberry jam for dipping.

"The perfect place to stay in Ogunquit"

We spent a week this past October at the Trellis House, and plan to repeat our trip in 2017--adding the rest of our family. The hosts, Laurence and Glen, prepare scrumptious breakfasts every morning, and are ready and willing to make dinner reservations and supply any other needs or requests a guest might have. It is the perfect place to stay!

English Muffin Bread

2 Loaves

The Trellis House loves to make Eggs Benedict but we are always running out of space to store English Muffins. Luckily, we also love to bake and now worry no more.

6 cups all-purpose flour
2 packages active dry yeast
1/4 cup sugar
1 teaspoon salt
1/2 teaspoon baking soda
2 1/2 cups warm milk
1/2 cup warm water
2 tablespoons fresh herbs or 1/2 cup grated Parmesan
   (optional)
cornmeal for dusting pans

Preheat oven to 400° and butter or spray 2 loaf pans and dust with cornmeal.

In a large bowl of a standing mixer using a dough hook blend 3 cups of flour with the yeast, sugar, salt, and baking soda. Add warm milk and water. Mix until smooth. Gradually add remaining flour (and herbs or cheese or both). A stiff dough will form. Knead the dough for 3 or 4 minutes.

Divide dough between the two prepared pans. Allow the bread to rise for 45 minutes and then bake 20-25 minutes. Let cool for 5 minutes and then remove from pans, place on a rack and let cool completely.

Signature Coffee Cake

2 Loaves

At The Trellis House we must have the perfect breakfast coffee cake! This is our signature recipe and we couldn't be more proud of it. We adapt the recipe by adding 2 cups of blueberries, raspberries, diced apples, or any fruit that is at its peak and it is perfect each time. This recipe can be made up ahead and refrigerated or frozen before baking...a real time-saver!

Streusel:

1/3 cup packed light brown sugar

1/3 cup granulated sugar

1/3 cup all-purpose flour

4 tablespoons butter softened

1 tablespoon ground cinnamon

1 cup finely chopped pecans or walnuts

Cake:

3 cups all-purpose flour plus 1 tablespoon to toss with berries

1 tablespoon baking powder

1 teaspoon baking soda

1 teaspoon ground cinnamon

1/4 teaspoon salt

1 3/4 cups sour cream room temperature

1 cup light brown sugar

1 cup granulated sugar

3 large eggs room temperature

7 tablespoons butter melted and cooled

2 cups fresh blueberries (or other fruit) sorted and stemmed

For the streusel: Using your fingers, mix brown sugar, granulated sugar, flour, butter, and cinnamon together in bowl until mixture resembles wet sand. Stir in pecans.

Adjust oven rack to middle position and heat oven to 350°. Butter two 9-inch square cake pans. Whisk flour, baking powder, baking soda, cinnamon, and salt together in a large bowl. In separate bowl, whisk together sour cream, brown sugar, granulated sugar, eggs, and melted butter until smooth. Gently fold egg mixture into flour mixture until smooth. Toss blueberries or other fruit with one tablespoon of flour and then fold into batter. Scrape batter equally into prepared pans, smooth tops, and sprinkle with topping.

Gently tap pans on counter to settle batter. Bake cakes until tops are golden and puffed, and toothpick inserted in centers comes out with few crumbs attached, 25-30 minutes, rotating pans halfway through baking. Let cakes cool in pans for 30 minutes. Serve slightly warm or at room temperature.

To make ahead: Portion batter and topping into cake pans but do not bake. Wrap cake pans tightly with plastic wrap and refrigerate for up to 1 day, or freeze for up to 1 month. Bake cakes as directed, increasing baking time to 30-35 minutes if refrigerated, or 40-45 minutes if frozen (do not thaw cakes before baking).

Popovers with Honey Butter

Serves 12 Popovers

1 1/2 tablespoons unsalted butter melted
Extra softened butter for greasing pans
1 1/2 cups flour
3/4 teaspoon kosher salt
3 extra-large eggs at room temperature
1 1/2 cups milk at room temperature

Preheat the oven to 425°.

Generously grease 12 popover pans or Pyrex custard cups with softened butter. Place the pans in the oven for exactly 2 minutes to preheat. Meanwhile, whisk together the flour, salt, eggs, milk, and melted butter until smooth. The batter will be thin. Fill the popover pans just less than half full and bake for exactly 30 minutes. Do not peek. Turn popovers out and serve immediately.

For the Honey Butter: Use a fork to mix 1 stick of softened butter in a small bowl with 1 tablespoon honey. Spoon into a ramekin and chill slightly until ready to serve.

Blueberry Coffee Cake Muffins with Cinnamon Butter

16 Muffins

These muffins rock! They are handsome devils and are perfect with coffee as a first course.

12 tablespoons unsalted butter at room temperature
1 1/2 cups sugar
3 large eggs at room temperature
1 1/2 teaspoons vanilla
1 cup sour cream
1/4 cup buttermilk
2 1/2 cups all-purpose flour
2 teaspoons baking powder
1/2 teaspoon baking soda
1/2 teaspoon kosher salt
2 half-pints fresh blueberries picked through for stems
A sprinkle of turbinado or sanding sugar

Preheat oven to 350°. Place 16 paper liners in muffin pans and spray only the top of the pan so muffins are easier to get out.

In the bowl of an electric stand mixer fitted with a paddle attachment, cream the butter and sugar until light and fluffy, about 5 minutes. With the mixer on low speed, add the eggs one at a time, then add the vanilla, sour cream, and buttermilk. In a separate bowl, sift together the flour, baking powder, baking soda, and salt. With the mixer on low speed add the flour mixture to the batter and beat until just mixed. Fold in the blueberries with a spatula and be sure the batter is completely mixed.

Scoop the batter into the prepared muffin pans (I use an ice cream scoop so muffins are a uniform size), filling each cup just over the top. Bake for 25-30 minutes, until the muffins are lightly browned on top and cake tester comes out clean. Transfer to a wire rack to cool. Sprinkle with turbinado or sanding sugar. Serve with cinnamon butter.

For the Cinnamon Butter: Use a fork to mix 1 stick of softened butter in a small bowl with 1 teaspoon each of cinnamon and honey. Spoon into a ramekin and chill slightly until ready to serve.

Peach Streusel Cake

1 Cake

Peach pie is my favorite pie of all time and so we adapted this coffee cake recipe to include peaches as well. Honestly, we find fresh peaches are annoying to work with and turn mushy so use frozen peaches which work perfectly every time.

Streusel:
1/2 cup all-purpose flour
1/4 cup packed light brown sugar
1/4 teaspoon salt
3 tablespoons unsalted butter softened
1 cup chopped toasted pecans

Batter:
2 cups all-purpose flour
1 teaspoon baking powder
1 teaspoon baking soda
1/2 teaspoon salt
1 stick unsalted butter softened
1 cup sugar
2 large eggs
1 cup sour cream
2 teaspoons vanilla
1 - 10-ounce bag frozen peaches coarsely chopped

Preheat the oven to 325° and butter and flour a 9-inch spring form pan.

For the streusel: In a bowl, using your fingers, combine the flour, brown sugar, and salt. Add the butter and mix until incorporated. Mix in the pecans.

In a bowl, whisk the flour, baking powder, baking soda and salt. In a large bowl, beat the butter and sugar at medium-high speed until light, 3 minutes. Beat in the eggs 1 at a time; beat in the sour cream and vanilla. Add the dry ingredients and beat at low speed until incorporated. Spread two-thirds of the batter in the pan. Fold the peaches into the remaining batter and spoon into the pan. Scatter the streusel crumbs on top.

Bake the cake for 1 hour and 30 minutes, or until a toothpick inserted in the center comes out clean; loosely cover the cake with foil for the last 15 minutes of baking. Transfer to a rack and cool for 30 minutes, then remove the ring and let the cake cool completely before serving.

Cranberry Bread
with Cranberry Butter

1 Loaf

There are times when a homey cranberry bread is required to remind guests that fall is coming in New England. This bread is citrusy and delicious. We serve this with cranberry butter.

2 cups all-purpose flour
1/2 teaspoon salt
1/2 teaspoon baking soda
1 1/2 teaspoons baking powder
1 cup sugar
2 teaspoons grated lemon zest
2 teaspoons grated orange zest
1/4 cup fresh lemon juice
1/4 cup fresh orange juice
2 tablespoons butter
1/4 cup water
1 large egg beaten
2 teaspoons pure vanilla extract
1 1/2 cups fresh cranberries chopped
1 cup walnuts or pecans chopped

Preheat oven to 350°. Prepare a standard loaf pan by spraying with vegetable oil.

Sift together the flour, salt, baking soda, baking powder, and sugar in a large bowl. In a saucepan add the zests, juices, butter, and water. Stir and bring to a boil. Pour liquid mixture into flour and stir slightly, then add egg and extract and stir until blended. Fold in cranberries and walnuts. Pour batter into prepared pan and bake for 50- 60 minutes until a pick inserted comes out clean. Let cool for 5 minutes and then remove to wire rack and let cool completely. Serve with cranberry butter.

For the Cranberry Butter: Use a fork to mix 1 stick of softened butter in a small bowl with 1 tablespoon cranberry relish and 1 teaspoon sugar. Spoon into a ramekin and chill slightly until ready to serve.

Make Ahead Streusel Mix

6 Cups

We use streusel on many of our muffins and baked goods and even on pancakes and waffles. We keep this on hand always. It's a wonderful way to save time; just keep a bag on hand in the freezer and use as needed.

1 cup packed brown sugar
1 cup granulated sugar
1 cup flour
12 tablespoons butter cut into 1/2-inch pieces and chilled
3 tablespoons ground cinnamon
3 cups finely chopped walnuts or pecans

Using fingers, combine brown sugar, granulated sugar, flour, butter, and cinnamon in bowl until mixture resembles coarse meal. Stir in nuts. Freeze in zipper-lock bag for up to 2 months.

Monster Cinnamon Buns

12 Servings

These rolls are beautiful and enormous. They make a statement and are exactly what an indulgent, buttery, billowy, frosted cinnamon roll should be.

Dough:
3/4 cup (1 1/2 sticks) unsalted butter
1 cup milk
3/4 cup plus 1 teaspoon sugar
1 1/4 teaspoons salt
3 envelopes active dry yeast
1/2 cup warm water
5 eggs
8 1/2 - 9 1/2 cups flour

Filling:
5 cups brown sugar firmly packed
1 1/4 cups (2 1/2 sticks) unsalted butter
3 tablespoons cinnamon

Frosting:
8 ounces cream cheese softened
1/4 cup heavy cream
1 teaspoon vanilla
3 to 4 cups confectioners' sugar sifted

For the dough: Heat the butter with the milk, 3/4 cup of the sugar and the salt in the saucepan until butter is melted. Set aside to cool. In a large mixing bowl, sprinkle the yeast over the warm water, add the remaining teaspoon sugar, stir and set aside for 10 minutes until the mixture is bubbly. Add the butter and milk mixture and the eggs and beat until well combined. Add the flour a cup at a time using enough flour to form a stiff dough.

Turn out on a floured board and knead until smooth and satiny, about 10 minutes (or knead in mixer with a dough hook until sides are clean), about 5 minutes. Place dough in a very large buttered bowl, turn to butter the top and allow to rise, covered loosely with a kitchen towel until doubled in bulk, about 1 hour. Punch the dough down and roll out to a large rectangle, 24x36 inches. Butter 2 - 9x13 inch glass baking dishes.

For the filling: Beat together the brown sugar, butter, and cinnamon until well combined. Spread evenly over the surface of the dough. Roll up length-wise and cut into 2-inch-wide slices to make 12 rolls. Place 6 rolls in each buttered dish. Cover loosely with a kitchen towel and allow to rise until doubled in bulk, about 1 hour.

Preheat oven to 350°. Bake the rolls for about 20-30 minutes or until puffed and browned. Cool to room temperature in the baking pan on a rack.

For the frosting: Beat the cream cheese, cream, and vanilla until well combined. Add the confectioners' sugar and beat until smooth and soft, not stiff. Frost the rolls and serve immediately.

Custard Filled Cornbread

1 Loaf

Ok, admittedly this is a weird recipe. However, it's magic! It's been around for a lot longer than The Trellis House and for good reason. When the cornbread is done, there is a creamy custard in the middle and our guests are always puzzled how we got it in there!

2 large eggs
3 tablespoons melted butter
3 tablespoons sugar
1/2 teaspoon salt
2 cups whole milk
1 1/2 tablespoons white vinegar
1 cup all-purpose flour
3/4 cup yellow cornmeal
1 teaspoon baking powder
1/2 teaspoon baking soda
1 cup heavy cream

Preheat the oven to 350° and butter an 8-inch square pan. Put the pan in the oven to get hot while making the batter. Using a fork stir the flour, cornmeal, baking powder and soda together in a bowl until fluffy. In a separate bowl using a mixer, blend the eggs and melted butter. Add the sugar, salt, milk, and vinegar and beat well. Add the dry ingredients and mix until the batter is smooth. You don't want lumps in this cornbread.

Pour the batter into the heated pan and then pour the cream into the center. Don't even think about stirring! Bake for 1 hour or until golden. Cut into squares and serve warm with honey for happiest guests.

———•◦•———

MAPLE NUT MUFFINS

8 Muffins

When we want a simple but beautiful muffin we go to these buttery, maple scented cakes which have no sugar but taste delightful and make the house smell like breakfast in Maine should smell.

1 3/4 cups all-purpose flour
2 teaspoons baking powder
1 teaspoon baking soda
1/2 teaspoon salt

1/2 cup walnuts chopped medium
1/2 cup unsalted butter
3/4 cup maple syrup
1/2 teaspoon maple extract
1 cup sour cream
1 large egg

Preheat oven to 400°. Spray a large muffin pan and insert paper liners. In a bowl sift together dry ingredients and then add nuts and stir. Beat butter in an electric mixer until light and airy. Slowly add the syrup and extract and beat well. Mix in the sour cream and egg until well blended. Add the dry ingredients and mix just until blended. Do not over mix. Fill muffin cups to the top and bake about 15 minutes. Muffins are cooked when a toothpick inserted in the center comes out clean or with moist crumbs attached. Transfer to a wire rack to cool. Serve with maple butter.

For the Maple Butter: Use a fork to mix 1 stick of softened butter in a small bowl with 1 tablespoon maple syrup. Spoon into a ramekin and chill slightly until ready to serve.

"Customer service BEYOND expectation!!!"

I am not one to over-state or over-exaggerate
but a truly incredible experience! Glen and
Laurence do a remarkable job at making you
feel welcome and comfortable at the Trellis
House! Hands down the greatest customer
service anywhere I have ever experienced
at any place I have ever stayed! Great food
(breakfast), great accommodation, great
attention to detail, great people. Thank you
for everything Laurence and Glen as well as
Bentley (terrific dog). 100 percent the place to
book in Ogunquit!!!

FIRST COURSES
&
STARTERS

When we first bought The Trellis House we believed we could handle anything that our new business could throw at us. There was one thing, however, that gave me nightmares, that in my mind's eye I couldn't imagine how we were going to handle and that was: "How on earth am I going to be able to prepare and offer unique fruit dishes every morning?" Terrifying! I literally stopped and said this out loud several times a day during the 6-month renovation period. We have solved the problem though as you can see.

THE
TRELLIS HOUSE
FIRST COURSES AND STARTERS

Homemade Granola Parfait
with Honey Crème and Fresh Fruit

Baked Apple Cranberry Oatmeal Brŭlée

Grapefruit Brûlée with Vanilla Crème

Fresh Fruit with Vanilla Dip

Blueberry Banana Overnight Oatmeal

Fruit Salad with Champagne Mint Syrup

Strawberries Filled with Vanilla
Mascarpone

Watermelon with Vanilla Crème and
Grahams

Berry Granola Crème Brûlée

Homemade Granola Parfait with Honey Crème and Fresh Fruit

8 Servings

Our homemade granola has become a signature breakfast item at The Trellis House. For such a simple dish, you wouldn't believe the compliments we get and the happiness this parfait imparts. The combination of flavors is perfect and rarely a bite is ever left in a parfait glass.

Signature Granola:
1/2 cup vegetable oil
1/4 cup honey
1/2 cup maple syrup
1/4 cup brown sugar
2 tablespoons vanilla
1/4 teaspoon ground ginger
1/4 teaspoon cinnamon
4 cups old fashioned oats
3/4 cup dry roasted slivered almonds
1/2 cup sunflower seeds
1/2 cup shredded coconut
3/4 cup chopped pecans
1/2 cup dried cranberries
1/2 cup raisins

1/2 cup chopped dates
1/2 cup chopped apricots

Honey Yogurt:
1-quart Greek yogurt
1 teaspoon vanilla
1 tablespoon honey

Fruit Salad:
1 pint strawberries cut into small chunks
1 pint blueberries
1 large apple peeled, cored and chopped
1 large orange peeled, segmented and chopped
or any combination of fruit that appeals to you

For the granola: Preheat oven to 300°. In a large bowl whisk together first 7 ingredients. Add the next 5 ingredients and stir until well coated. Spread onto two parchment lined baking sheets and shake pans or use your hands to get an even layer. Bake for about 40 minutes, stirring occasionally until golden. Do not over bake and check often during the last 10 minutes so the granola doesn't burn. Let granola cool completely and then add the last 4 ingredients, stir to combine. Granola will last for two weeks on the counter in an airtight container or longer in zip-lock bags in the freezer. Makes 10 cups.

For the honey-yogurt: Whisk yogurt, vanilla, and honey in a medium bowl until combined. Refrigerate until ready to use.

For the fruit salad: Wash and prepare fruit. Stir together in a bowl and let sit at room temperature until ready to use.

To assemble the parfaits: Use 8 parfait glasses. Measure 1/4 cup granola into each glass. Carefully spoon 2 tablespoons of yogurt and then 1 heaping tablespoon of fruit. Repeat each layer. Finish with a small dollop of yogurt. Sprinkle with granola and top with a sprig of mint.

Baked Apple Cranberry Oatmeal Brûlée

8 Servings

Sure to be an eye opener. This, I am often told, is what oatmeal should be.

2 2/3 cups old fashioned oats
1/2 cup brown sugar
2 medium apples peeled and diced
2/3 cup dried cranberries or raisins
1 teaspoon cinnamon
1/2 teaspoon salt
1/2 stick butter melted

additional brown sugar for brûlée
heavy cream
mint sprigs

Preheat oven to 375°. Stir all ingredient together in an oven proof baking dish that has been buttered or sprayed with vegetable oil. Bake for 1 hour and then spoon into individual serving bowls. Sprinkle a couple of teaspoons of brown sugar on top and use a kitchen torch to brûlée. Serve with a small splash of cream on top and garnish with a mint leaf or two.

Grapefruit Brûlée
with Vanilla Crème

8 Servings

Pink grapefruit with caramelized sugar and some sweetened yogurt is a combination that cannot be underestimated. The reaction of our guests each time we serve this is unbeatable.

4 pink grapefruits cut in half
1/2 cup Greek yogurt
splash of pure vanilla extract
drizzle of honey
8 teaspoons turbinado sugar
8 Maraschino cherries cut in half

Mix yogurt, vanilla, and honey with a fork in a bowl and refrigerate until ready to use. Slice a bit off each end of the grapefruit so that each half sits flat. Cut each grapefruit in half horizontally and place each in a small bowl. Sprinkle with 1 teaspoon or so of sugar and caramelized with a kitchen torch. Spoon a small amount of the yogurt mixture onto each half to cover the center and top with a cherry.

Fresh Fruit
with Vanilla Dip

2 Cups

I once had this dip at a neighbor's Christmas Party. Honestly, I don't generally love eating fruit but I couldn't get enough of the incredible combination of apples, strawberries, pears, and this fabulous dip. Use any fruit you like. It's all good.

1 - 16-ounce container sour cream
1 package vanilla instant pudding
1/3 cup pineapple juice
apples sliced
pears sliced
strawberries halved
banana slices
kiwi sliced
assorted melon large dice
pineapple chunks

Mix all together and chill. Place fruit decoratively on a beautiful plate or small dish. Put a dollop of "dip" on top or in a ramekin on the side. This can be served on a large platter on a buffet or individually for a first course. Garnish with mint sprigs, of course.

Blueberry Banana Overnight Oatmeal

12 Servings

When I know we are going to have a late night or precious little time in the morning we prepare these wonderful layered oatmeal parfaits.

6 cups old fashioned rolled oats
6 cups whole milk
2 tablespoons pure vanilla extract
1 cup brown sugar
3 cups blueberries sorted and stemmed
3 ripe bananas medium diced
12 teaspoons turbinado sugar
mint sprigs for garnish

Stir together oats, milk, vanilla, and brown sugar in a large bowl until well mixed. Spoon into a large container with a lid and place in refrigerator overnight. In the morning, when ready to serve, cut up bananas and then layer oatmeal mixture, berries, and bananas in as many layers as your parfait glass will hold in amounts that suit your liking.

We use old fashioned glass canning jars. Once jars are filled sprinkle 1 teaspoon of sugar over top and use a kitchen torch to caramelize the sugar for a delicious crunchy top. Garnish with mint leaves.

Fruit Salad with Champagne Mint Syrup

16 Servings

How can we make fruit salad more interesting? Champagne works. The simple syrup made with bubbles adds a delicate undertone to fruit salad.

Syrup:
1/2 cup champagne or sparkling wine
1/2 cup sugar
2 tablespoons finely chopped fresh mint leaves

Berry Salad:
1 cantaloupe peeled and seeded and cut into 1 inch dice
1 honeydew peeled and seeded and cut into 1 inch dice
1 pint raspberries
1 pint blueberries
1 pint strawberries hulled and diced
1 pint blackberries
2 or 3 peaches pitted and diced

Stir the champagne, sugar, and mint in a saucepan and bring to a simmer for about 10 minutes until syrupy. Strain into a jar. Use any combination of fresh, ripe fruit you like and pour syrup over and mix well. Serve in individual glass dishes or bowls. You may not use all the syrup; use only what is needed to get the fruit just sweet enough. Garnish with mint and serve.

Strawberries Filled with Vanilla Mascarpone

8 Servings

Our guests are astonished by the elegance of this simple, glorious garnish or first course.

1 cup Mascarpone cheese
1/2 cup heavy cream
3 tablespoons confectioners' sugar
1/4 teaspoon pure vanilla extract
1 teaspoon orange zest
1 vanilla bean split lengthwise seeds scraped out
16 large fresh strawberries

Combine all ingredients except for strawberries in the bowl of a stand mixer and whip until soft peaks form. Scrape the mixture into a pastry bag fitted with a star tip.

Cut the green leaves off the strawberries so each strawberry stands flat. With a small sharp knife cut an x in each berry cutting three-quarters of the way to the bottom. Gently spread each berry apart to form four petals.

Fill each strawberry carefully with cream and refrigerate or serve immediately.

Watermelon with Vanilla Crème and Grahams

8 Servings

What to do with watermelon? How can we make watermelon interesting and delicious enough to be served as a first course? These are the things that keep me up at night.

1 small ripe watermelon
1 cup plain Greek yogurt
1 tablespoon instant vanilla pudding mix
4 Graham crackers

Cut the rind off the watermelon and discard. Dice watermelon into 1 inch cubes and refrigerate until ready to use. Mix Yogurt and pudding mix together.

Spoon watermelon into cups or bowls, drizzle with yogurt mixture and then crush a half of a Graham cracker over each serving. Garnish with a mint sprig and serve.

Berry Granola Crème Brûlée

8 Servings

We wanted a fresh berry starter that also had crunch and was delicious. Voila!

2 cups plain Greek yogurt
1/2 teaspoon pure vanilla extract
1 teaspoon honey
2 pint fresh berries: blueberries, strawberries, blackberries, etc., cleaned or hulled as needed
2 teaspoons fresh lemon juice
4 cup homemade granola (see master recipe page 66)
8 teaspoons turbinado sugar

Mix the yogurt, vanilla, and honey and refrigerate until ready to use. Put the berries in a small saucepan, add 1/4 cup water, and simmer until just softened. Add sugar to sweeten depending on ripeness of fruit. Stir in lemon juice and remove from heat.

Divide the fruit among 8 ramekins. Top with granola. Fill the ramekins to the top with yogurt and use a knife to smooth the top. Sprinkle each ramekin with 1 teaspoon of turbinado sugar and caramelize using a kitchen torch. Garnish with a mint leaf.

"An Ogunquit Gem"

I debated whether or not to write a review because in true selfishness, I want to keep Glen, Laurence, and the Trellis House to my very own. The Trellis House has (somewhat) recently gone through a major renovation and I assure you that the transformation is amazing. Based upon the B&B's I researched, the Trellis House is unlike most inn's in Ogunquit. Modern features, beautiful and tasteful decor, fabulous hosts, and and an all around feeling that you don't want to leave, EVER. Breakfast was absolutely amazing. AMAZING! The inn is intimate and and the perfect size. 8 stunning rooms, each uniquely decorated and so perfect. And the bed, shall I say is quite comfortable and with linens that you would expect to find at a 5 star hotel (perhaps even better). If you want a quiet little place to stay at, that is conveniently located in between Perkins Cove and town, then you should look no further. We will be back to the Trellis, and we will be bringing friends.
You should go too!

PANCAKES, FRENCH TOAST
& WAFFLES

We generally alternate breakfast

each day between

savory and sweet,

egg and pancake

and waffle dishes.

What I love about this category

is that it's somewhat like baking

and I can get so much more creative

than with eggs.

THE
TRELLIS HOUSE

PANCAKES, FRENCH TOAST & WAFFLES

Almond Croissant French Toast
with Almond Praline Crunch

Bananas Foster French Toast
with Whipped Cream Cheese

Ham and Swiss Croissant French Toast
with Maple Dijon Syrup

Pecan Crunch Waffles with Molasses Butter

Brûléed Orange Challah French Toast

Pineapple Upside Down Pancakes
with Pineapple Maple Syrup

THE
TRELLIS HOUSE

PANCAKES, FRENCH TOAST & WAFFLES

Strawberries and Mascarpone Stuffed
French Toast with Pecan Crust

Best Buttermilk Pancakes

Pumpkin Waffles with Molasses Butter

Carrot Cake Pancakes with
Maple Cream Cheese Drizzle

Blueberry Blintz Pancakes

Silver Dollar Pecan Pie Pancakes

Almond Croissant French Toast with Almond Praline Crunch

8 Servings

When we want to totally impress our guests, which is every day, this dish hits every note. Try it and it will change your life and make people swoon.

French Toast:
8 large croissants sliced in half
4 large eggs
2 egg yolks
1 tablespoon brown sugar
1 1/2 cups half & half
1/4 teaspoon almond extract
1/4 teaspoon pure vanilla extract

Almond Praline Crunch:
1 tablespoon butter
1 cup sliced almonds
1 tablespoon sugar

For the almond croissant French toast: Cut the croissants in half lengthwise and place on a baking sheet, uncovered in the oven overnight to dry out.

In the morning whisk together the eggs, yolks, sugar, half and half, vanilla, and almond extract.

For the almond praline crunch: Melt butter in a small saucepan over medium heat. Add the almonds and sugar and sauté until golden, about 10 minutes, stirring constantly. Be careful not to overcook as they go from golden to burnt easily. Remove from heat and set aside.

Heat a large skillet or griddle with 2 tablespoons butter. Submerge each croissant half in the egg mixture for about 10 seconds, any longer and the croissant will fall apart. Carefully place the croissant on the griddle cut side down and cook until golden brown and a crust has formed. Flip and cook until the bottom is golden brown too. Repeat with remaining croissants. Place two half croissants cut side up on a plate, sprinkle with confectioner's sugar and top with a heaping tablespoon of almond praline crunch.

Bananas Foster French Toast with Whipped Cream Cheese

8 Servings

Ok, yes, we agree this is ridiculous and we are not sorry!

French Toast:
3 large eggs
4 egg yolks
2 tablespoons granulated sugar
1 cup whole milk
1/2 cup heavy cream
1 teaspoon cinnamon
1 teaspoon pure vanilla extract
butter for frying
canola oil for frying
8 slices brioche or challah cut on the diagonal
    in generous 1 inch slices.

Bananas Foster Topping:
4 tablespoons butter
1 cup light brown sugar
pinch cinnamon
2 ripe bananas sliced
2 tablespoons banana liqueur
1/4 cup dark rum

Whipped Cream Cheese:

3 ounces cream cheese room temperature

1 teaspoon pure vanilla extract

1/2 teaspoon orange zest

1 cup very cold heavy cream

Whisk together the eggs, yolks, sugar, milk, cream, cinnamon, and vanilla. Heat 1 tablespoon each of the butter and canola oil in a large frying pan or griddle until the butter is sizzling and the oil is shimmering. Place 3 slices of the bread in the custard mixture and let soak on both sides for about 30 seconds. Lift bread out and let the mixture mostly drain off. Cook for about 2 minutes on each side until golden brown and crisp on the edges. Repeat with remaining bread slices.

For the bananas: Heat the butter over high heat until melted. Whisk in the sugar and cinnamon and cook until the sugar has melted and the mixture has slightly thickened. Add the bananas and cook until slightly softened. Add the banana liqueur and rum and cook until the alcohol has burned off, about 2 minutes.

For the whipped cream cheese: Put cream cheese, vanilla, and orange zest in the bowl of a stand mixer fitted with a whisk and whip until light and fluffy. Slowly add the cream and whip until soft peaks form. Refrigerate until ready to use.

Serve 2 slices of French toast per person topped with the banana syrup, a dollop of whipped cream cheese, and a sprinkling of confectioners' sugar.

Ham and Swiss Croissant French Toast with Maple Dijon Syrup

8 Servings

You have heard me say many times throughout this cookbook that something is my favorite. Well a ham and swiss croissant truly is my favorite breakfast item. I love them more than life itself. This recipe was created to take our favorite breakfast item over the top and then over the top again. You can truly die happy with this one, and here is the recipe.

8 croissants
8 slices good country ham
8 slices swiss cheese
6 eggs
1 cup half & half
1 cup whole milk

1 tablespoon Dijon mustard
1/2 teaspoon salt
additional dijon mustard for croissant tops

Maple Dijon syrup:
1 stick butter
1/3 cup brown sugar
1/3 cup maple syrup
2 tablespoons Worcestershire sauce
2 tablespoons Dijon mustard

Spray a 13 x 9 baking dish with nonstick spray. Cut croissants in half. In a large bowl whisk eggs, half & half, and milk, 1 tablespoon of mustard, and salt. Submerge and soak the bottom of each croissant in the egg mixture until soft and place in baking dish, cut side up. Place a slice of ham and cheese on top, folding in half if needed to fit the bottom croissant. Spread a very thin layer of mustard on each croissant top and dip in the egg mixture until soft then place a top on each sandwich. Pour any remaining egg mixture over croissants. Cover with plastic wrap and let soak overnight.

Preheat oven to 350° and bake for about 25 minutes until golden.

For Maple Dijon Syrup: Meanwhile, in a saucepan, mix butter, brown sugar, maple syrup, Worcestershire, and Dijon mustard. Bring to a boil and then lower the heat and simmer for a few minutes. Drizzle generously over each croissant before serving.

Pecan Crunch Waffles with Molasses Butter

6 Waffles

Waffles don't generally get people excited but these aren't just any waffle. The pecan meal in the batter gives them a crunch and density while the waffle is light and fluffy. Simple, rustic and delicious.

2 large eggs
1 3/4 cups buttermilk
1/2 cup (1 stick) butter melted and cooled to room temperature
2 teaspoons vanilla extract
1 3/4 cups all-purpose flour
2 tablespoons sugar
2 teaspoons baking powder
1 teaspoon baking soda
1 teaspoon salt
1/2 cup pecan meal

In a medium sized mixing bowl beat together the eggs, buttermilk, melted butter, and vanilla. In a separate bowl whisk together the dry ingredients.

Combine the wet and dry ingredients, stirring just until nearly smooth; a few small lumps may remain.

Spray your waffle iron with a non-stick cooking spray before preheating it. For an 8" round waffle iron, use about 1/3 cup batter; cook for 4-6 minutes or until the iron stops steaming. Place waffle on plate and smear with molasses butter.

For the Molasses Butter: Use a fork to mix 1 stick of softened butter in a small bowl with 1 tablespoon molasses. Spoon into a ramekin and chill slightly until ready to use.

Brûléed Orange Challah French Toast

4 Servings

We use thick slices of challah dipped in a rich egg and cream batter and then spoon orange syrup over the top. Although we serve maple syrup on the side it rarely gets used.

3 large eggs
4 egg yolks
1 cup whole milk
1/2 cup heavy cream
1 teaspoon grated orange zest
1/4 cup orange juice
2 tablespoons packed light brown sugar
2 tablespoons plus 8 teaspoons sugar
2 teaspoons pure vanilla extract
1 tablespoon orange liqueur such as Grand Marnier
8 day old slices challah 3/4 inch thick
butter for frying
canola oil for frying

Orange Glaze:
1/2 cup orange juice
1/2 cup orange marmalade
2 tablespoons butter cold and cut into small pieces

Whisk together the eggs, yolks, milk, cream, zest, juice, brown sugar, and two tablespoons granulated sugar, vanilla, and orange liqueur until combined.

Heat a large skillet or griddle with 1 tablespoons each butter and canola oil. Soak the bread slices in the egg mixture until completely soaked through, 15 to 30 seconds per side. Cook on the griddle cut side down and cook until golden brown and a crust has formed. Flip and cook until the bottom is golden brown too. Repeat with remaining bread slices and place on a baking sheet.

Sprinkle each French toast with a teaspoon of sugar. Using a kitchen torch flame the sugar in small circles until the sugar melts and lightly browns. Serve 2 slices of French toast per guest with orange syrup on top.

For the glaze: Heat the orange juice and marmalade in a saucepan on medium heat and stir continuously until it comes to a simmer. Turn the heat down to low and add the butter, stir until melted. Return to a simmer for a few minutes but be careful not to let it boil.

Pineapple Upside Down Pancakes with Pineapple Maple Syrup

6 Servings

At The Trellis House, we take our pancakes very seriously and we think this pancake delivers. We use our best pancake recipe and add sunny pineapple and some sugar to create a twist on pancakes.

1 Recipe Best Buttermilk Pancakes (See page 96)
2 cups diced pineapple

Pineapple maple syrup:
1 cup pure maple syrup
4 tablespoons cold butter cut into pieces
1/2 cup diced pineapple
3 tablespoons sugar

For the syrup: Bring the maple syrup to a light simmer in a saucepan. Whisk in the butter, one piece at a time until thickened. Stir in 1/2 cup of the pineapple and remove from heat. Cover to keep warm.

Make buttermilk pancake recipe.

Heat a nonstick skillet or griddle over medium heat. Add

1 tablespoon butter and 1 teaspoon canola oil and brush to coat the skillet bottom evenly. Pour batter in 1/4 cup portions and cook until bubbles appear. Spoon a couple of tablespoons of pineapple over each pancake and then sprinkle the pineapple with a teaspoon or so of sugar. When the undersides are golden brown with crispy edges, flip the pancakes and cook for a minute or two more until the pineapple is caramelized and the pancakes are cooked. Repeat with remaining batter, stack and drizzle with pineapple maple syrup.

Strawberries and Mascarpone Stuffed French Toast with Pecan Crust

8 Servings

This is one of our favorite breakfasts to serve. Crunchy, sublime, sweet and savory, our guests are always asking for the recipe.

Filling:

1 pint fresh strawberries

1 pint mascarpone or cream cheese room temperature

1 tablespoon sugar

1 teaspoon vanilla

French toast:

8 slices day old brioche or challah cut on the diagonal
   in generous 1 inch slices

3 large eggs

4 egg yolks

2 tablespoons granulated sugar

1 cup whole milk

1/2 cup heavy cream

1 teaspoon cinnamon

1 teaspoon pure vanilla extract

2 cups finely chopped pecans

butter for frying

canola oil for frying

For the strawberry filling: Hull and slice or dice the strawberries. Place in a stand mixer and blend the mascarpone, strawberries, sugar, and vanilla until well incorporated.

Cut a pocket in each slice of bread but do not cut all the way though. Use your fingers to widen the pocket slightly. Fill each bread slice with about a tablespoon of the strawberry mixture.

Excluding the butter, oil, bread, and pecans, whisk remaining ingredients together in a bowl. Place pecans in a shallow pie plate.

Heat a large skillet or griddle with 1 tablespoons butter and 1 teaspoon canola oil. Soak the filled bread slices in the egg mixture until completely soaked through, 15 to 30 seconds per side. Press 1 side of each soaked bread slice into the pecans and place pecan side down on griddle.

Cook on the griddle until golden brown and a crust has formed. Flip and cook until the bottom is golden brown too. Repeat with remaining bread slices. Dust with confectioners' sugar, garnish with sliced strawberries and serve.

Best Buttermilk Pancakes

10 Pancakes

When we say "best" we mean it. This is our go-to light, fluffy, tender, and flavorful pancake recipe. We serve these as is and as the basis for many of our creative pancake breakfasts.

2 cups buttermilk
1 large egg
3 tablespoons butter melted and cooled
2 cups all-purpose flour
2 tablespoons sugar
2 teaspoons baking powder
1/2 teaspoon baking soda
1/2 teaspoon salt
butter and canola oil for griddle

Whisk the flour, sugar, baking powder, baking soda, and salt in a medium bowl to combine. Whisk the egg and melted butter into the buttermilk until combined. Make a well in the center of the dry ingredients in the bowl; pour in the milk mixture and whisk very gently until just combined (a few lumps should remain). Do not over mix.

Heat a nonstick skillet or griddle over medium heat. Add 1 tablespoon butter and 1 teaspoon oil and brush to coat the skillet bottom evenly. Pour batter in 1/4 cup portions and cook until bubbles appear and underside is golden brown with crispy edges, about 3 minutes. Flip the pancakes and cook for a minute or two more until golden and just cooked through. Repeat with remaining batter, stack and serve immediately.

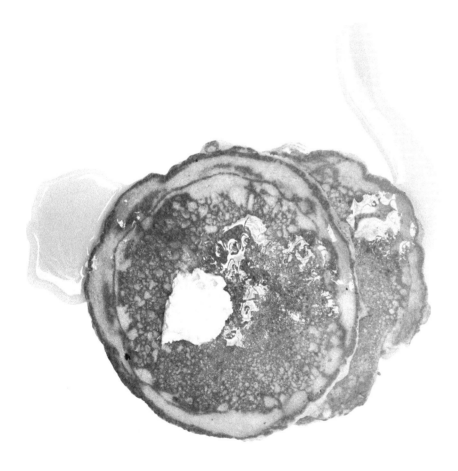

Pumpkin Waffles with Molasses Butter

6 Waffles

We wanted a fall waffle and tried many recipes which included pumpkin but none of them delivered a light, fluffy pumpkin flavored pancake and then I realized that canned pumpkin muted the taste of the spices. Here is our delicious pumpkin waffle with no pumpkin!

2 large eggs
1 3/4 cups buttermilk
8 tablespoons butter melted and cooled to room
   temperature
2 teaspoons pumpkin pie spice
1 3/4 cups all-purpose flour
2 tablespoons sugar
2 teaspoons baking powder
1 teaspoon baking soda
1 teaspoon salt
1/2 cup pecan meal (whole pecans finely ground in
   food processor)

In a medium-sized mixing bowl, beat together the eggs, buttermilk, melted butter, and vanilla. In a separate bowl whisk together the dry ingredients. Combine the wet and dry ingredients, stirring just until nearly smooth; a few small lumps may remain. Spray waffle iron with a non-stick cooking spray before preheating it. Use about 1/3 cup batter and cook until the batter stops steaming. Plate and then dust with confectioners' sugar.

For the Molasses Butter: Use a fork to mix 1 stick of softened butter in a small bowl with 1 tablespoon molasses. Spoon into a ramekin and chill slightly until ready to serve.

Carrot Cake Pancakes with Maple Cream Cheese Drizzle

4 Servings

This is one of Glen's favorites and I love making them for him. This recipe tastes just like the real thing!

1 1/2 cups flour
1/4 cup sugar
1 tablespoon baking powder
1/2 teaspoon baking soda
1 teaspoon pumpkin pie spice
2 large eggs
1 1/2 cups buttermilk
3 tablespoons melted butter
1/2 teaspoon pure vanilla extract
1 cup finely grated carrots patted dry with paper towels
1 teaspoon grated orange zest
1/4 cup toasted pecans or walnuts finely chopped
3 ounces cream cheese room temperature
1 cup pure maple syrup

In the large bowl of an electric stand mixer, whisk together the flour, sugar, baking powder, baking soda, and pumpkin pie spice. Whisk together the eggs, buttermilk, butter, vanilla, carrots, and orange zest in another bowl. Add to the flour mixture and whisk until just combined. Fold in the pecans. Cover and refrigerate for 30 minutes.

For the maple cream cheese drizzle:
Combine the cream cheese and maple syrup in an electric stand mixer fitted with a whisk attachment and whip for about 1 minute until combined.

Heat a nonstick skillet or griddle over medium heat. Add 1 teaspoon oil and brush to coat the skillet bottom evenly. Pour batter in 1/4 cup rounds and cook until bubbles appear and undersides are golden brown with crispy edges, about 3 minutes. Flip the pancakes and cook for a minute or two more until golden and just cooked through. Repeat with remaining batter, stack, drizzle with maple cream cheese and sprinkle with additional toasted nuts. Serve immediately.

Blueberry Blintz Pancakes

8 Pancakes

I loved blintzes as a child and still do. The traditional crepe filled with sweet farmer's cheese and typically served with sour cream and cooked fruit has been transformed into a pancake with very similar qualities and taste. These are the most unique and delicious pancakes we have ever eaten.

4 eggs lightly beaten
1 tablespoon sugar
1 cup cottage cheese
1 cup sour cream
1 cup flour
1/2 teaspoon baking soda
3/4 teaspoon salt
1 squeeze lemon juice
1 teaspoon vanilla
1/2 pint fresh blueberries

Beat eggs and then stir in cottage cheese, sour cream, vanilla and lemon juice until smooth. Sift dry ingredients into the liquid mixture and stir gently until just incorporated (do not over beat or pancakes will be tough). Let stand a few minutes while heating skillet with butter or vegetable oil. Drop batter in 1/4 cup rounds onto skillets sprinkle generously with blueberries, and cook until bubbles appear and underside edges are very golden. Flip and continue cooking until steam disappears, approximately 3 minutes. Pancakes should be firm to the touch or they may be under cooked in the middle. Stack and garnish with blueberries and sprinkle with confectioners' sugar.

Silver Dollar Pecan Pie Pancakes

6 Servings

Pecan Pie for breakfast would be unthinkable. So we disguised our pancakes! Pecans and maple syrup give them their nutty crunch and that irresistible pecan pie flavor.

1 Recipe Best Buttermilk Pancakes (See page 96)

2 cups finely chopped pecans toasted and divided
2 cups pure maple syrup
1 tablespoon molasses
4 tablespoons butter cut into pieces

Add 1 cup of finely chopped pecans to the "Best Buttermilk Pancake" recipe and let sit for 15 minutes while you make the maple syrup butter.

For the pecan maple syrup: Bring the maple syrup and molasses to a light simmer in a saucepan. Whisk in the butter, one piece at a time until thickened. Stir in 1 cup of the pecans and remove from heat. Cover to keep warm.

Heat a nonstick skillet or griddle over medium heat. Add 1 teaspoon oil and brush to coat the skillet bottom evenly. Pour portions of 2 tablespoons of batter onto griddle and cook until bubbles appear and undersides are golden brown with crispy edges, about 2 minutes. Flip the pancakes and cook for a minute or two more until golden and just cooked through. Repeat with remaining batter, stack high and spoon pecan maple syrup on top.

EGG DISH
FAVORITES

Eggs are a major component

in our lives at The Trellis House.

We use an average of 300 eggs per week!

The challenge with eggs is that

there are so many choices,

but the following recipes are

the most elegant and in some cases,

represent the simplest way to show our

commitment to great food for breakfast.

As I often say in the kitchen as we are

cooking eggs, "not too many wiggles"!

THE
TRELLIS HOUSE
EGG DISH FAVORITES

Signature Eggs Benedict with Roasted Tomatoes
and Good Bacon

Master Recipe Easy Lemony Hollandaise Sauce

Master Recipe Poached Eggs

Breakfast Burritos with Avocado, Bacon,
and Cheddar

Lobster and Sausage Hash Benedict

A Fine Breakfast Sandwich

Master Recipe for Quiche Lorraine

Bird in the Nest

Pizza for Breakfast

THE
TRELLIS HOUSE
— · —
EGG DISH FAVORITES

Frittata with Roasted Vegetables and Feta

Corned Beef Hash with Baked Eggs

Scrambled Egg and Cheese Muffins with Sausage

Florentine Eggs Benedict with
Goat Cheese Spread

Breakfast Strata with Sausage, Mushrooms,
and Monterey Jack

Breakfast Strata with Potatoes, Rosemary,
and Fontina

Breakfast Bake

Sausage and Cheese Egg Pouf

Signature Eggs Benedict with Roasted Tomatoes and Good Bacon

4 Servings

Our guests deserve the very best and this version of Eggs Benedict is one of our proudest breakfasts to serve. I personally don't care for Canadian bacon but love the combination of eggs, roasted tomatoes, good bacon, and lemony Hollandaise. Honestly, people who say they don't like Eggs Benedict tell us we have converted them.

1 Recipe Easy Hollandaise Sauce (See recipe page 112)
1 Recipe Poached Eggs (See recipe page 113)

2 large beefsteak tomatoes cut into 8 thick slices
8 large eggs
8 slices good quality thick cut bacon cooked until crisp
   and broken in half
4 Wolferman's english muffins toasted and buttered
chopped chives for garnish

Preheat oven to 400°. Place sliced tomatoes on a baking sheet, drizzle lightly with olive oil and season with salt and pepper. Roast for about 30 minutes until tomatoes are very soft with a few brown spots starting to show. Remove from oven; they will keep warm until ready to use.

Meanwhile, lay bacon slices on a rack placed on a baking sheet lined with foil and cook along with tomatoes until brown and crisp, about 30 minutes.

Make the Easy Hollandaise sauce. Toast and butter english muffins. Top each muffin half with a slice of roasted tomato, 2 half slices of bacon, a poached egg and a tablespoon or so of Hollandaise. Garnish with chopped chives and a sprinkle of Paprika.

Master Recipe Easy Lemony Hollandaise Sauce

Makes 1 Cup

3 large egg yolks at room temperature
1 lemon juiced
1 stick butter
1/8 teaspoon white pepper
1 or 2 tablespoons hot water

Place yolks in blender and process on low for 15 seconds. Melt the butter in a saucepan until very hot. With the blender on low, drizzle in the butter through the small clear insert on cover of blender and blend for 30 seconds, until the sauce is very thick. With blender still running squeeze in lemon being careful not to let any seeds fall in. Add white pepper and check consistency. Add water if needed; sauce should be light and slightly thicker than the consistency of heavy cream (it should not be pudding or paste like). Serve immediately or keep for up to an hour at room temperature and just before serving add a tablespoon of very hot tap water and whisk.

Master Recipe
Poached Eggs

Fill a large saucepan with water and 1 tablespoon of white vinegar and bring to a gentle simmer. Break an egg into a cup and slip it into the simmering water, repeat with rest of eggs and cook 3-4 minutes until there are no wiggles but yolk is still runny. Remove eggs with slotted spoon and use immediately or transfer to a bowl of warm water until ready to serve.

Breakfast Burritos
with Avocado, Bacon
and Cheddar

8 Servings

This recipe is without a doubt one of our top five recipes which elicits moans of delight. Shockingly, many of our guests have never had a burrito and often try to tell me (gently) that they would prefer an alternative dish. I always ask them to, please, just try it. Although burrito is a foreign word, all the ingredients are exactly what one would want from a traditional breakfast, creamy scrambled eggs, sharp cheddar cheese, savory sausage etc. Add refried beans, and it never fails to delight with the delicious combination these ingredients produce. I love my "I told you so!" moment.

8 large flour tortillas
1 can refried beans
8 breakfast sausage links
2 cups grated sharp cheddar cheese
16 large eggs
1/2 cup sour cream
1/2 teaspoon kosher salt
1/4 teaspoon black pepper
2 tablespoons butter
2 ripe avocados pitted and sliced or diced

Slice sausages into ½ inch discs and fry in a pan until cooked through and golden brown. Set aside. Heat refried beans in microwave, covered in plastic wrap, until hot. Set aside.

Whisk eggs, sour cream, salt, and pepper together in a medium bowl. Heat butter in skillet on medium until foamy. Add eggs, and using a spatula, stir slowly until eggs begin to set. Do not overcook eggs. Remove from heat and set aside.

For burrito assembly: Heat a tortilla on a hot skillet for a few seconds on both sides until pliable. Spread a tablespoon or so of beans on the tortilla and then top with

¼ cup cheese, ¼ cup sausage slices, ¼ cup scrambled eggs, and one or two avocado slices. Fold in the sides and roll tortilla up. (Youtube it if you can't figure it out.)

On a hot, buttered griddle, cook each burrito, turning once so both sides are golden. Serve with a dollop of sour cream with store bought salsa on the side. Delish!

Lobster and Sausage Hash Benedict

8 Servings

Every visitor to Maine must have lobster for breakfast at least once. I had a similar dish while brunching in Fort Lauderdale and sought to recreate it at home. We combine the best of both worlds, buttery lobster meat, garlicky sausage, crispy hash browns, and roasted vegetables all served with a poached egg with lemony hollandaise drizzled over the top.

For the hash:
1 - 20-ounce bag shredded hash brown potatoes thawed
4 tablespoons butter
2 tablespoons vegetable oil
1 green pepper cut into 1/2-inch dice
1 red bell pepper cut into 1/2-inch dice
1 large red or white onion cut into 1/2-inch dice
1 pound breakfast or Italian sausage sliced into 1/2 inch pieces
1 teaspoon salt
1/2 teaspoon black pepper
1 teaspoon onion powder
1 teaspoon garlic powder
1 pound cooked fresh lobster meat cut into large chunks
fresh chopped chives for garnish

1 Recipe Easy Hollandaise Sauce (See page 112)
1 Recipe Poached Eggs (See page 113)

Use the largest griddle or sauté pan that you have. Over medium-high heat cook sausages until well browned and cooked through, remove from griddle, and set aside. Add butter and oil to the griddle and cook potatoes and vegetables, flipping occasionally, until potatoes are well browned and vegetables are cooked, about 20 minutes. Season with salt, pepper, onion and garlic powder. Add cooked sausage back into the hash. Push hash to the side of the griddle to make room to sauté the lobster. Melt two tablespoons additional butter on the griddle and sauté lobster chunks until warmed through. Place a generous portion of hash on each plate and then top with lobster and poached eggs. Drizzle with Hollandaise and garnish with chives and a sprinkle of Paprika.

A Fine Breakfast Sandwich

4 Servings

One of my favorite breakfast items of all time is a bacon, egg, and cheese sandwich on a grilled and buttered "hard" roll or Kaiser roll as it is also known. There is just something about this combination that always works. Of course, we had to take it to the next level by making our own cheddar-herb biscuits and roasting thick slices of locally grown beefsteak tomatoes.

1 Recipe Cheddar Herb Biscuits (page 30) or English Muffin Bread (page 42) or go ahead and use English Muffins but make sure they are Wolferman's or I can't talk to you anymore.

1 large beefsteak tomato cut into 4 thick slices
8 large eggs
1/2 cup sour cream
1/2 teaspoon kosher salt
1/4 teaspoon black pepper
2 tablespoons butter
4 slices sharp cheddar cheese
4 slices thick cut good quality bacon
1 small bunch chives chopped fine

Place tomato slices on baking sheet. Drizzle with olive oil and salt and pepper. Bake in a 400° oven for about 30 minutes until very soft and spotty brown.

Meanwhile. lay bacon slices on a rack placed on a baking sheet lined with foil and cook along with tomatoes until brown and crisp, about 30 minutes.

Whisk eggs, sour cream, salt, and pepper together in a medium bowl. Heat butter in skillet on medium until foamy. Add eggs and using a rubber spatula stir slowly until eggs begin to set. Lower heat and continue cooking until eggs are nearly set, do not overcook. Remove from heat and season with salt and pepper.

Split each biscuit and place on a griddle with butter until golden or toast and butter bread if using. Place bottom of each biscuit on a plate. Lay a slice of cheese, a roasted tomato slice, two bacon halves, and 1/4 of the scrambled eggs on each. Lay second biscuit half or slice of toast on top, perpendicular to sandwich and garnish plate lightly with more chives.

Master Recipe for Quiche Lorraine

6 Servings

This is our go-to recipe for the quintessential brunch staple from Cook's Illustrated. Our quiche must be creamy and savory and full of flavor. Here are our favorites.

1 master recipe for 8 or 9-inch prebaked pie shell
  (see page 123)
8 ounces good quality bacon cut into 1/2 inch pieces
2 large eggs plus 2 yolks
1 cup whole milk
1 cup heavy cream
1/2 teaspoon salt
1/2 teaspoon white pepper
pinch grated nutmeg
1/2 cup gruyere cheese grated

Adjust oven rack to center position and heat oven to 375°. Fry bacon in skillet over medium heat until crisp and brown, about 5 minutes. Transfer with slotted spoon to paper towel-lined plate. Meanwhile, whisk all remaining ingredients except cheese in medium bowl. If the pie shell has been previously baked and cooled, place it in the preheating oven for about five minutes to warm it, taking care that it does not burn.

Spread cheese and bacon evenly over bottom of warm pie
shell and set shell on oven rack. Pour in custard mixture
to 1/2-inch below crust rim. Bake until lightly golden
brown and a knife blade inserted about one inch from the
edge comes out clean, and center feels set but soft like
gelatin, 32-35 minutes. The center of the quiche will be
surprisingly soft when it comes out of the oven, but the
filling will continue to set as it cools.

Crabmeat Quiche:

Follow Master Recipe for Quiche Lorraine, above, reducing quantities of milk and cream to 3/4 cup each. Add 2 tablespoons dry sherry and a pinch of cayenne pepper to custard mixture. Substitute 8 ounces (1 cup) cooked crabmeat tossed with 2 tablespoons chopped fresh chives for bacon and cheese.

Leek and Goat Cheese Quiche:

Sauté white part of 2 medium leeks, washed thoroughly and cut into 1/2- inch dice (about 2 cups), in 2 tablespoons unsalted butter over medium heat until soft, 5-7 minutes. Follow Master Recipe for Quiche Lorraine, above, reducing quantities of milk and cream to 3/4 cup each. Omit bacon; substitute 4 ounces mild goat cheese, broken into 1/2-inch pieces, for Gruyere. Add leeks with cheese.

Zucchini and Cheddar Quiche:

Slice 2 zucchini into 1/2-inch pieces and sauté in butter until tender. Season with salt and pepper. Follow Master Recipe for Quiche Lorraine, above, reducing quantities of milk and cream to 3/4 cup each. Omit bacon; substitute 1 cup good quality cheddar. Add zucchini and cheese.

Master Recipe Single 9 Inch Pie Crust

1 Crust

1 1/4 cups all-purpose flour
1/2 teaspoon salt
1 tablespoon sugar
6 tablespoons unsalted butter chilled and cut into 1/4 inch pieces
4 tablespoons all-vegetable shortening chilled
3-4 tablespoons ice water

Mix flour, salt, and sugar in food processor fitted with steel blade. Scatter butter pieces over flour mixture, tossing to coat butter with a little flour. Cut butter into flour with five 1-second pulses. Add shortening and continue cutting in until flour is pale yellow and resembles coarse cornmeal with butter bits no larger than small peas, about four more 1-second pulses.

Turn mixture into medium bowl. Sprinkle 3 tablespoons of ice water over mixture. With blade of rubber spatula, use folding motion to mix. Press down on dough with broad side of spatula until dough sticks together, adding up to 1 tablespoon more ice water if dough will not come together. Shape dough into ball with your hands, then flatten into 4-inch-wide disc. Dust lightly with flour, wrap in plastic, and refrigerate for 30 minutes before rolling to 1/8 inch thickness, about the height of two stacked quarters.

Bird in the Nest

1 Serving

When a guest is unable (or unwilling) to try our breakfast menu, this simple dish we all may remember from our childhood always fits the bill. My mom used to make this for me when I had a cold or just pretended to. Crispy, buttery bread with an egg cooked in the middle makes everyone happy.

1 slice country or rustic white bread 3/4 inch slices
1 tablespoon butter
1 large egg
salt and fresh ground pepper

Cut a 2-inch circle out of the center of the bread (I use a cookie cutter). Heat the butter in a non-stick skillet over medium heat. Add the bread slice (and the cut-out bread circle next to it) and cook until golden brown, about 2 minutes. Turn the bread over and break the egg into the hole. Sprinkle with salt and pepper. Cook for about 3 minutes until the underside of the bread is golden brown and the egg white is set. Remove the bread circle and set aside. Turn the bread (and egg) once again and cook for another minute or two until the yolk is cooked as desired. Serve immediately with the bread circle for dipping.

"Charming place, wonderful hosts"

We stayed for a weekend, in the Arbor room. The room is just as it appears in pictures, small, clean, and ADORABLE. Very nice bed and plenty of space to store our things. The bathroom is clean and had a small frig (nice surprise). The grounds are fabulous, providing nice little spots to sit and relax. Inside you will find the same. A number of comfortable places to sit and enjoy. Afternoon snacks are a fun way to meet other guests. Breakfast is top-notch, and it's obvious the hosts, Laurence and Glen, love what they do, and are good at it! Very gracious, and accommodating to all. Located right off Marginal Way. Perfect for early morning, sunrise walks. There are many restaurants in walking distance too.

Pizza for Breakfast

4 Servings

Need I say more...

2 balls homemade pizza dough (see recipe page 153
   or store bought)
2 tablespoons olive oil
1 - 8 ounce container crème fraîche or ricotta
2 tablespoons fresh parsley minced
2 tablespoons fresh chives minced
1 tablespoon fresh basil minced
2 tablespoons butter divided
1 Vidalia or red onion sliced thin
1/2 pound good quality bacon or sausage diced
8 large eggs
2 cups grated sharp cheddar divided

Preheat oven to 400°. Whisk together the crème fraîche
(or ricotta) and herbs in a small bowl and season with salt
and pepper. Refrigerate until ready to use.

Divide the dough into 4 individual balls and roll out as thin
as possible into individual pizzas. Brush pan and each pizza
lightly with oil, lightly season with salt. Place pizzas on
baking sheets and bake until lightly golden brown, about
10 minutes.

Cook bacon or sausage over medium high heat until crisp/cooked. Drain on a paper towel, reserving 1 tablespoon of the fat. Cook the onion in the fat with a pinch of sugar until caramelized, about 20 minutes.

Spread a thin layer of creme fraiche on each pizza and then sprinkle cheese on top, saving 1/2 cup cheese for the scrambled eggs. Sprinkle bacon and onion over each. Bake for about 5 minutes while you make the scrambled eggs.

Heat a tablespoon of butter in a large sauté pan and whisk the eggs. Cook slowly, stirring constantly with a rubber spatula until large curds form. Add the cheese and continue cooking and stirring until eggs are set. Do not overcook. Season with salt and pepper.

Divide the eggs on each pizza and garnish with more cheese and herbs.

FRITTATA WITH ROASTED VEGETABLES AND FETA

6 Servings

This beautiful, individual Frittata nearly takes up the whole plate! Everyone complains that it is too much food but we can't help but spoil our guests with this spectacularly presented, puffy winner of a dish.

Egg Mixture:

18 large eggs

1/2 cup sour cream

1/2 cup milk

1 teaspoon kosher salt

1/2 teaspoon black pepper

Roasted Vegetables:

3 tablespoons extra virgin olive oil

1 medium red onion medium diced

2 small zucchini cut in half and then sliced crosswise

1 red bell pepper large dice

1 yellow bell pepper large dice

8 ounces white button mushrooms sliced thinly

1 pint cherry tomatoes cut in half

salt and pepper

1 cup feta crumbled

1 cup good quality extra sharp cheddar shredded

torn basil or chopped chives

Preheat oven to 425°. Place all vegetables on a baking sheet and use your hands to toss with oil and salt, and pepper. Roast for about 30 minutes, shaking the pan occasionally until some vegetables begin to become golden and spotty brown. Do this in advance. Meanwhile whisk eggs, sour cream, milk, salt, and pepper together until blended.

Preheat broiler. You can use one large skillet but we use individual 6-inch oven proof sauté pans. If using individual sauté pans, heat 2 or 4 at a time, and to each, add about 1 teaspoon of butter and about 1/3 cup of vegetables (or all the eggs and veggies if making one large Frittata). Get the pan(s) good and hot so the veggies begin to sizzle. Lower heat and using a ¾ cup measure, pour egg mixture into each individual pan or skillet. Cook, gently stirring, and lifting eggs allowing liquid under the cooked portions until Frittata is beginning to set.

Remove from heat and sprinkle a three-finger pinch of each cheese onto each Frittata. Place in oven about 6 inches from broiler and bake until eggs are very puffed and almost completely set, about 4-6 minutes. The top should be golden in some areas. Slide Frittata onto a plate, pretty cheese side up and scatter basil or chives on top. Serve immediately for presentation purposes as it deflates soon after it comes out of the oven.

CORNED BEEF HASH WITH BAKED EGGS

6 Servings

1 - 20 ounce bag frozen diced potatoes
1 tablespoon vegetable oil
4 slices good quality bacon chopped into pieces
1 onion finely chopped
2 garlic cloves minced
1/2 teaspoon fresh minced thyme
1/3 cup heavy cream

1/4 teaspoon hot sauce
12 ounces corned beef thinly sliced and chopped
6 large eggs
salt and pepper

Stir potatoes, oil, 1/2 teaspoon salt, and 1/4 teaspoon black pepper in a bowl. Cover with plastic wrap and microwave for 5 minutes

Cook bacon in a 12-inch non-stick skillet over medium heat until fat begins to render, about 3 minutes. Stir in onion and cook until softened and lightly browned, about 10 minutes.

Stir in garlic and thyme, hot potatoes, cream, and hot sauce. Gently pack potatoes into pan with a spatula and cook for a few minutes undisturbed. Flip hash over in sections and repack lightly into pan. Cook and flip occasionally until mixture is nicely browned. Stir in corned beef and heat through.

Preheat oven to 400. We use individual cast iron skillets but you can use one large one. Spray skillet(s) with vegetable oil and heat over medium flame. Spoon hash into skillets and make a small indentation in middle or make 6 indents in the hash in a large skillet. Add 1 egg in each indentation and season with salt and pepper. Place pan(s) in oven and bake until eggs are cooked through but yolks are still runny, about 4 or 5 minutes.

Scrambled Egg and Cheese Muffins with Sausage

12 Muffins

On occasion, we have a breakfast buffet at The Trellis House, and these muffins are among the offerings. This is a wonderful way to serve eggs, without really serving eggs. These are also great on-the-go so when we have guests who need to depart before breakfast, although rare, we can send them on their way with one of these travelling breakfasts.

4 ounces (½ package) bulk breakfast sausage broken
  into pieces
24 Ritz crackers coarsely crushed
10 large eggs
1/3 cup half & half
1 cup grated sharp cheddar
4 scallions sliced thin

Adjust oven rack to lower-middle position and heat oven
to 450°. Spray 12 cup muffin tins with baking spray.
Microwave sausage in an uncovered bowl until fat renders,
about 1 minute. Drain. In a separate bowl, whisk crackers,
eggs, and half and half together until incorporated. Stir in
cheddar, scallions, and sausage.

Pour egg mixture with a ladle into muffin tins. Bake until
tops are set and lightly golden, about 10 minutes, rotating
pan halfway through. Let, muffins cool slightly, then use a
small knife to loosen and remove from pan. Serve hot or at
room temperature.

Florentine Eggs Benedict with Goat Cheese Spread

4 Servings

We wanted a twist on Eggs Benedict that we could serve when we had vegetarian guests and devised this recipe that is truly unique and delicious.

1 Recipe Poached Eggs (See page 113)
1 Recipe Easy Hollandaise Sauce (See page 112)

2 boxes frozen chopped spinach
4 tablespoons butter divided
salt and pepper to taste
1 cup goat cheese
1 tablespoon chopped chives
1 teaspoon lemon juice
salt and pepper

2 large beefsteak tomatoes cut into 8 thick slices
8 large eggs
4 Wolferman's english muffins toasted
chives for garnish

Preheat oven to 400°. Place sliced tomatoes on a baking sheet, drizzle lightly with olive oil and season with salt and pepper. Roast for about 30 minutes until tomatoes are very soft with a few brown spots starting to show. Remove from oven, they will keep warm until ready to use.

Mix goat cheese, 2 tablespoons butter, lemon juice, chives, salt, and pepper to taste in a small bowl until combined. Set aside until ready to use.

Make Hollandaise sauce.

Microwave thawed spinach in a covered bowl just until warm. Place in a large, clean kitchen towel and wring out most of the liquid; return to bowl, stir in 2 tablespoons of butter and season generously with salt and pepper. Taste the spinach mixture and if it isn't delicious add more butter.

Toast English muffins. Spread goat cheese mixture evenly among toasted muffins. Top with a slice of roasted tomato, 1/4 cup of the spinach mixture, a poached egg, and then top with a tablespoon or so of Hollandaise. Garnish with chopped chives and a sprinkle of paprika.

Breakfast Strata with Sausage, Mushrooms and Monterey Jack

6 Servings

I hate breakfast casseroles! Well I love them but I hate serving them for breakfast at The Trellis House and vowed to never do it because it seems so ... well ... uninspired and lacking effort. Then I found a few recipes from Cook's Illustrated that we think elevate the humble casserole and warrant a place in our repertoire. The next two recipes are our favorites.

8-10 slices supermarket French bread
3 tablespoons unsalted butter softened
8 ounces bulk breakfast sausage crumbled
3 medium shallots minced
8 ounces white button mushrooms cleaned and quartered
1/2 cup dry white wine such as sauvignon blanc
1 1/2 cups grated Monterey jack cheese
6 large eggs
1 3/4 cups half and half
2 tablespoons minced fresh parsley

Adjust oven rack to middle position and heat oven to 325°. Arrange bread in single layer on large baking sheet and bake until dry and crisp, about 40 minutes, turning slices over halfway through drying time. (Alternatively, leave slices out overnight to dry.) When cooled, butter slices on one side with 2 tablespoons butter; set aside.

Fry sausage in a nonstick skillet over medium heat, breaking sausage apart with wooden spoon, until sausage has lost raw color and begins to brown, about 4 minutes; add shallots and cook, stirring frequently, until softened and translucent, about 1 minute longer. Add mushrooms to skillet, and cook until mushrooms no longer release liquid, about 6 minutes; transfer mixture to medium bowl and season to taste with salt and pepper. Add wine to skillet, increase heat to medium-high, and cook until reduced to 1/4 cup, 2 to 3 minutes; set aside.

Butter an 8-inch square baking dish with remaining 1 tablespoon butter; arrange half the buttered bread slices, buttered-side up, in single layer in dish. Sprinkle half of sausage mixture, then 1/2 cup grated cheese evenly over bread slices. Arrange remaining bread slices in single layer over cheese; sprinkle remaining sausage mixture and another 1/2 cup cheese evenly over bread. Whisk eggs and parsley in medium bowl until combined; whisk in reduced wine, half-and-half, 1 teaspoon salt, and pepper to taste.

Pour egg mixture evenly over bread layers; cover surface flush with plastic wrap, and refrigerate at least 1 hour or up to overnight.

Remove dish from refrigerator and let stand at room temperature 20 minutes. Meanwhile, adjust oven rack to middle position and heat oven to 325°. Uncover strata and sprinkle remaining 1/2 cup cheese evenly over surface; bake until both edges and center are puffed and edges have pulled away slightly from sides of dish, 50-55 minutes. Cool on wire rack 5 minutes; serve.

Breakfast Strata with Potatoes, Rosemary and Fontina

6 Servings

Still hate serving breakfast casseroles.... but boy is this a good one.

8-10 slices supermarket French bread
5 tablespoons unsalted butter softened
salt and freshly ground black pepper
2 medium new potatoes cut into 1/2 inch cubes
3 medium shallots minced

2 medium cloves garlic pressed

1 1/2 teaspoons minced fresh rosemary

1/2 cup dry white wine such as sauvignon blanc

1 1/2 cups shredded fontina cheese

6 large eggs

1 3/4 cups half & half

2 tablespoons minced fresh parsley

Adjust oven rack to middle position and heat oven to 325°. Arrange bread in single layer on large baking sheet and bake until dry and crisp, about 40 minutes, turning slices over halfway through drying time. (Alternatively, leave slices out overnight to dry.) When cooled, butter slices on one side with 2 tablespoons butter; set aside.

Bring 1 quart water to boil in medium saucepan over medium-high heat; add 1 teaspoon salt and boil potatoes until just tender when pierced with tip of paring knife, about 4 minutes; drain potatoes.

Heat 2 tablespoons butter in medium nonstick skillet over medium heat and cook potatoes until just beginning to brown, about 10 minutes. Add shallots and cook, stirring frequently, until softened and translucent, about 1 minute longer; add garlic and rosemary and cook until fragrant, about 2 minutes longer. Transfer mixture to medium bowl; season to taste with salt and pepper and set aside. Add wine to skillet, increase heat to medium-high, and cook until reduced to 1/4 cup, 2 to 3 minutes; set aside.

Butter an 8-inch square baking dish with remaining 1 tablespoon butter; arrange half the buttered bread slices, buttered-side up, in single layer in dish. Sprinkle half of potato mixture, then 1/2 cup grated cheese evenly over bread slices. Arrange remaining bread slices in single layer over cheese; sprinkle remaining potato mixture and another 1/2 cup cheese evenly over bread. Whisk eggs and parsley in medium bowl until combined; whisk in reduced wine, half-and-half, 1 teaspoon salt, and pepper to taste. Pour egg mixture evenly over bread layers; cover surface flush with plastic wrap, and refrigerate at least 1 hour or up to overnight.

Remove dish from refrigerator and let stand at room temperature 20 minutes. Meanwhile, adjust oven rack to middle position and heat oven to 325°. Uncover strata and sprinkle remaining 1/2 cup cheese evenly over surface; bake until both edges and center are puffed and edges have pulled away slightly from sides of dish, 50-55 minutes (or about 70 minutes for doubled recipe). Cool on wire rack 5 minutes; serve.

"WONDERFUL!!! "

My husband an I stayed for a couple of days and
it was simply wonderful. We were celebrating
our anniversary and they went above an beyond
to make our stay comfortable and pleasant.
Their pup-pup Bentley was such a love, very
well mannered an friendly. Glen greeted us
and started us off with a couple of glasses of
champagne... Delicious!
Their breakfast menu was very unique
and delicious as well!!!
Glen brought us bakery treats each night along
with an English Lemon cake for our anniversary!
They are just wonderful and make you feel
like long time friends. It's a beautiful bed and
breakfast. Your in the middle of both ends of
shops... One side is to Perkins Cove and the
other you come in on is Main Street....then
beach is right at the end of the street!
Can't say enough!!! But we will be
regulars for them!

Breakfast Bake

12 Servings

Ok, I know I said we don't serve breakfast casseroles at The Trellis House and we don't…usually. However, every B&B needs a simple overnight casserole recipe and this is ours.

2 packages bulk pork sausage
1 large green pepper chopped
1 medium onion chopped
3 cups frozen hash brown potatoes thawed
2 cups sharp cheddar cheese shredded
1 cup Bisquick
2 cups whole milk
1/4 teaspoon black pepper
4 large eggs

Butter rectangular baking dish, 13x9x2 inches. Cook sausage, bell pepper, and onion in 10-inch skillet over medium heat, stirring occasionally, until sausage is no longer pink; drain. Stir together sausage mixture, thawed potatoes and 1 1/2 cups of the cheese in baking dish.

In another bowl, stir Bisquick mix, milk, pepper, and eggs until blended. Pour into baking dish. Cover with plastic wrap if not being baked right away and refrigerate up to one hour or overnight.

Remove dish from refrigerator and allow to stand at room temperature for 20 minutes. Meanwhile, heat oven to 400°. Bake uncovered 40-45 minutes or until knife inserted in center comes out clean. Sprinkle with remaining cheese. Bake a few minutes longer or just until cheese is melted. Cool 5 minutes or longer, and cut into squares.

Sausage and Cheese Egg Pouf

8 Servings

This dish always thrills. We bake each pouf in individual cast iron skillets and they puff up golden and gorgeous. Our guests gasp with delight when one is placed in front of them. No one has ever guessed that the secret ingredient is Pillsbury crescent rolls!

2 packages Pillsbury crescent rolls separated into triangles (as god made them)
16 large eggs
1/2 cup sour cream
1 roll Jimmy Dean bulk sausage
1 large green pepper diced small
1 - 8 ounce package button mushrooms sliced
1 teaspoon kosher salt
1/2 teaspoon black pepper
2 cups good quality sharp cheddar cheese grated
chives as garnish

You will need eight 6-inch cast iron skillets sprayed with vegetable oil or eight 4 inch ramekins. Preheat oven to 400°. Separate crescent rolls into individual triangles along their perforations and lay one triangle in the bottom of each skillet, reshape them covering the bottom of the pan to make a "crust".

Cook sausage until browned and no longer pink. Add the green pepper and mushrooms and cook for about 5 minutes until very soft. Remove from heat. Divide mixture evenly and spoon into each skillet making an even layer over each crescent "crust".

Whisk eggs, sour cream, salt, and pepper together in a bowl. Ladle about 3/4 cup of egg mixture into each skillet and then sprinkle with a three-finger pinch of cheese.

Place skillets on 2 baking sheets and bake for about 15-20 minutes until puffed and golden brown.

HAPPY
HOUR

Happy Hour at the Trellis House

is a wonderful time for guests

to come together in the late afternoon

to enjoy a snack on our porch.

Some guests will read, others will

chat or relax, but most will play

with our Labradoodle Bentley.

By playing we mean Bentley will lounge

around with his head on your lap and

make you feel special ... until he pops up

and goes to visit someone else.

THE
TRELLIS HOUSE
HAPPY HOUR

Bruschetta with Red and Yellow Peppers,
Tomatoes, and Basil

Lobster or Shrimp Salad Rolls

Cuisinart Pizza Dough

Savory Pinwheels

Knorr Spinach Dip

Lemon Feta Pepper Dip

Perfect Picnic Deviled Eggs

THE
TRELLIS HOUSE
— · —
HAPPY HOUR

Roasted Shrimp with Cocktail Sauce

Spinach and Cheese Custard Squares

Tzatziki Cucumber Garlic Dip

Whipped Feta and Red Pepper Dip

Zucchini And Tomato Tart

Bruschetta with Red and Yellow Peppers, Tomatoes and Basil

16 Servings

Our dear friend Elizabeth Bierbaum, who is a fabulous cook with great instincts, once served this at a barbecue in Los Angeles when Glen and I first met over 20 years ago. I have been making it ever since. Fresh, summery, and totally delicious. The only problem with this recipe is that I get stressed out when someone is eating this on the sofa!

8-12 medium tomatoes seeded and diced
4 red bell peppers seeded and diced
4 yellow bell peppers seeded and diced
2 cups chopped fresh basil leaves
6 medium garlic cloves finely minced
1/2 cup olive oil
salt and pepper

Several french baguettes cut into ¼ inch slices
   on the diagonal
olive oil
salt and pepper
grated parmesan cheese

Preheat oven to 400°. Place bread slices on 2 baking sheets, brush both sides with oil and sprinkle lightly with salt, and pepper. Bake for about 15 minutes until light golden brown; turn bread slices over and continue baking until browned and crisp. Remove from oven and sprinkle with grated Parmesan.

Mix tomatoes, peppers, garlic, basil, and olive oil in a large bowl. Season with salt and pepper. Serve bruschetta in a large bowl on a large platter with the crisp bread slices piled high around it.

Lobster or Shrimp Salad Rolls

8 Rolls

Honestly there is no one who doesn't feel special when they see a large platter of stunning lobster or shrimp salad roll sandwiches waiting for them when they return from the beach for afternoon snack time. Additionally, if the weather turns chilly we also purchase local clam chowder from our favorite lobster shack and have it steaming in a crock pot with mugs and oyster crackers.

1 pound cooked fresh lobster meat or cooked shrimp diced
1/3 cup Hellman's mayonnaise plus additional if needed
1 rib celery finely minced
1 tablespoon chives finely minced
large pinch kosher salt
large pinch freshly ground black pepper
juice of 1/4 lemon
pinch paprika

8 dinner rolls split along the top

Combine lobster, mayonnaise, celery, chives, lemon juice, salt, and pepper. The mayonnaise should be added only until the salad is cohesive. Refrigerate mixture until well chilled. When ready to serve, fill each roll and serve dusted with a little paprika. At The Trellis House we serve these on a large silver platter.

Cuisinart Pizza Dough

2 Balls of Dough

Versatile Dough for Savory Pinwheels or Pizza

2 1/4 teaspoons active dry yeast
1 teaspoon sugar
1/2 cup very warm water
4 cups all-purpose flour
1 1/2 teaspoons kosher salt
1 tablespoon olive oil
1 cup cold water

In a 2-cup liquid measure, dissolve yeast and sugar in warm water. Let stand until foamy, about 3 - 5 minutes. Insert dough blade in work bowl of Cuisinart and add flour, salt, and olive oil. Add cold water to yeast mixture, and with machine running, pour liquid through small feed tube as fast as flour absorbs it until dough cleans sides of work bowl and forms a ball; not all liquid may be needed. Then process for 45 seconds to knead dough. Dough may be slightly sticky. Dust dough lightly with flour; transfer to a large plastic food storage bag, squeeze out air and seal top. Let rise in a warm place for about 45 minutes or refrigerate until ready to use and then let rise for about an hour.

Place dough on a lightly floured surface and punch down; let rest 5-10 minutes. Roll into desired crust sizes.

Savory Pinwheels

12 Pieces

We make these little bites regularly because they are full of flavor and easy and great at room temperature.

1 ball pizza dough (see recipe page 153)
1/4 cup tomato sauce
1 cup shredded mozzarella cheese
one package pepperoni slices
1/4 cup diced red onion
2 tablespoons basil chopped

Heat the oven to 400°. Line a baking sheet with parchment or nonstick baking mat. Dust the counter lightly with flour. Place the ball of pizza dough on top and firmly pat it into a rectangular shape. Using a floured rolling pin, roll out the dough as thin as possible, roughly 10 by 15 inches. If the dough starts to spring back as you roll, let it rest for a few minutes, then roll again.

Spread the tomato sauce evenly all over the dough, leaving an inch of clean border at the top. Sprinkle the cheese over the sauce, then scatter the pepperoni slices to cover, and distribute the onion and basil.

Starting at the long end nearest you, begin rolling up the dough. When you get to the top, pinch the dough closed along the seam. Use a sharp chef's knife to slice the long tube into 12 rolls. Use the flat of your knife or a pastry scraper to help transfer the rolls to the baking sheet, spacing the rolls a few inches apart. Tighten up the rolls as needed after transferring and tuck any toppings that fell out back between the folds.

If you're eager for pinwheels right away, bake them immediately. If you have a little time and like puffier, more bready rolls, let them rise at room temperature for 30-45 minutes, then bake until the cheese is bubbly and the rolls are turning golden on top, 12-15 minutes. Serve warm or at room temperature.

Knorr Spinach Dip

12 Servings

This is just the recipe on the Knorr box and I can't personally see any way to improve on it. Except of course if I added bacon, or horseradish, or shredded cheddar, or... Oh never mind.

1 packet Knorr vegetable soup/dip mix
1 cup Hellman's mayonnaise
1 cup sour cream
1 can water chestnuts drained and finely chopped
2 scallions sliced thinly
1 box frozen chopped spinach thawed and drained
1 large round sourdough loaf hollowed out to use as a bowl

Defrost spinach and place in a clean kitchen towel, squeezing out all excess liquid. Chop water chestnuts. Blend sour cream, mayonnaise, and soup mix in bowl. Add spinach, water chestnuts, and onions and mix thoroughly. Chill for about 2 hours.

Meanwhile, remove the top one-fourth of the sour dough loaf. Hollow out the interior and spoon in the dip when ready to serve.

Serve in the bread bowl along side fresh vegetables and crackers.

Lemon Feta Pepper Dip

3 Cups

This is one of the finest dips we make. It is lemony, creamy, tart, pleasingly spicy and addictive. I have been making it for many, many years and people always ask for this recipe.

8 ounces feta cheese
8 ounces cream cheese
3/4 cup plain Greek yogurt
1/3 cup bottled pepperoncini or banana peppers
1/2 cup scallions sliced
1/2 teaspoon lemon zest minced
1/2 teaspoon fresh ground black pepper
good olive oil

Place all ingredients except olive oil in a food processor and pulse until incorporated but not too smooth. Transfer to a serving bowl, drizzle with olive oil and more black pepper before serving. Fine to keep in the refrigerator for a couple of days and use as a spread on roast beef or cold lamb sandwiches. Just sayin...

Perfect Picnic
Deviled Eggs

24 Pieces

There is just something perfect about my deviled eggs, in my humble opinion.

1 dozen eggs
1/4 cup mayonnaise
1 teaspoon Dijon mustard
1 tablespoon pickle relish
1/2 teaspoon sugar
1/2 teaspoon onion powder
1 teaspoon white vinegar
a few dashes hot sauce
salt and black pepper
paprika for dusting

To make perfect hard boiled eggs: Place eggs in a large pot and cover with water by 1 inch. Bring to a full boil and then turn down heat and simmer uncovered for exactly 13 minutes. Remove pot from heat and drain water. Fill pot immediately with ice if you want to easily peel the shells from your eggs. Once cool, drain ice water and gently roll eggs against the inside of the pan until well cracked. Peel eggs, rinse and lay on a paper towel to dry.

Slice eggs in half lengthwise. Gently remove yolks with your hand or a small spoon and place in bowl. Add remaining ingredients and mash with a fork until smooth. Use a whisk to whip until light and fluffy, adding a bit more mayo if needed. It is important that you taste the filling and season with salt and pepper. Fill each egg half with a scoop of the filling. Place on a serving platter and dust with paprika.

Roasted Shrimp with Cocktail Sauce

16 Servings

Basically, this is great classic shrimp cocktail but roasting the shrimp makes them so much more flavorful. I found this in an Ina Garten cookbook and really like the simple twist on the shrimp.

2 pounds large shrimp peeled and deveined but with tails intact
salt and pepper
1/2 cup Heinz chili sauce
1/2 cup ketchup
3 tablespoons prepared horseradish
2 teaspoons lemon juice
1/2 teaspoon Worcestershire
1/4 teaspoon hot sauce
olive oil

Preheat oven to 400°. Place shrimp on baking sheet and drizzle with olive oil and season generously with salt and pepper. Bake for about 7 minutes until shrimp are pink and just firm and cooked through. Serve warm or chilled with dipping sauce.

Combine the chili sauce, ketchup, horseradish, lemon juice, Worcestershire sauce, and hot sauce. Serve as a dip with the shrimp. Refrigerate until ready to serve.

Spinach and Cheese Custard Squares

16 Servings

A very simple, elegant appetizer. Serve this with the Tzatziki, (page 162) or with nothing at all. So simple, and guests rave.

10 large eggs
2 cups small curd cottage cheese
2 cups Jack, cheddar, pepper Jack or any cheese grated
2 tablespoons flour
1/2 cup parmesan grated
1/2 teaspoon onion powder
2 packages frozen chopped spinach thawed and drained
1 small can diced green chilies

In a large bowl whisk eggs, cottage cheese, flour, 1 cup cheese, flour, onion powder, and parmesan until well blended. Squeeze as much liquid as possible from spinach by placing it in a clean kitchen towel and ringing the heck out of it. Stir spinach and green chilies into egg mixture and season with salt and pepper. Spread mixture in a sprayed shallow, 9x13 quart casserole. Sprinkle remaining 1 cup cheese evenly over the top. Bake in a 350° oven until custard is firm to touch in the center, 30-40 minutes. Let stand about 10 minutes, then cut into portions.

Note: Leave the flour out or replace with cornstartch for gluten free guests

Tzatziki Cucumber Garlic Dip

5 Cups

Perfect for dipping spanakopita, spinach puffs, fried zucchini, or potato pancakes, and even as a sauce on grilled lamb on pita. It is so versatile we use it almost every day.

4 cups plain Greek yogurt
2 hothouse cucumbers unpeeled and grated or chopped
2 tablespoons kosher salt
1 cup sour cream
1 garlic clove pressed or minced
2 tablespoons champagne vinegar
1/4 cup freshly squeezed lemon juice
2 tablespoons olive oil
2 tablespoons fresh dill minced
1/4 teaspoon freshly ground black pepper

Grate the cucumbers and toss with 2 tablespoons of salt. Place salted cucumber in a strainer set over another bowl. Place in refrigerator for a couple of hours so the cucumber can drain. Place yogurt in a large bowl. Squeeze as much liquid as possible from the cucumber with your hands and add the cucumbers to the yogurt. Mix in the sour cream, garlic, vinegar, lemon juice, olive oil, dill, and black pepper. Cover and refrigerate until ready to serve.

Whipped Feta and Red Pepper Dip

2 Cups

Dips, dips, dips. Try making a dip every day of your life. Lemme know how that goes.

1 - 24 ounce jar roasted red peppers drained, patted dry
    and diced small
1 garlic clove pressed
2 tablespoons red wine vinegar
2 tablespoons sugar
1/4 teaspoon red pepper flakes
1/4 teaspoon salt
8 ounces feta cheese crumbled
2 tablespoons extra virgin olive oil
2 teaspoons fresh lemon juice
1/4 teaspoon pepper

Combine red peppers, garlic, vinegar, sugar, pepper flakes and salt in a small bowl and set aside. Blend Feta, oil, lemon juice and pepper in food processor until smooth. Serve both mixtures side by side. Spread feta mixture on toast/crackers and top with pepper mixture.

Zucchini And Tomato Tart

6 Servings

This recipe has a few steps but is worth it. Use a store-bought pie crust if you want to save time. This is a stunning summer appetizer or side dish that cannot be beat.

Crust:
1 1/4 cups all-purpose flour
1 tablespoon sugar
1/2 teaspoon salt
6 tablespoons extra virgin olive oil
3 tablespoons ice water
1/2 cup grated parmesan cheese

Filling:
1 large zucchini sliced into 1/8-inch-thick rounds
1 large beefsteak tomato sliced into 1/8-inch-thick rounds
salt
2 tablespoons extra virgin olive oil
1 medium garlic clove pressed
1/2 cup ricotta cheese
1/2 cup grated parmesan cheese
1/2 cup grated mozzarella cheese divided
2 tablespoons fresh basil leaves chopped

For the crust: Spray a 9-inch tart pan with a removable bottom with vegetable oil. Pulse the flour, sugar, and salt together in a food processor until combined. Drizzle the oil over the flour mixture and pulse until the mixture resembles coarse sand, about 12 pulses. Add 2 tablespoons of the ice water and continue to process until some of the dough begins to clump into large pieces and no powdery bits remain, about 5 seconds. If powdery bits of flour remain, add the remaining tablespoon water and pulse to incorporate, about 4 pulses. The dough should have many little crumbs with a few large clumps.

Place all but 1/3 cup of the dough crumbs into the prepared tart pan and, using your hands, press the crumbs into an even layer over the tart pan bottom. Sprinkle the remaining 1/3 cup crumbs around the edge of the tart pan and press into a tidy crust edge, about 3/4 inch up the sides of the pan. Lay plastic wrap over the dough and smooth out any bumps. Freeze the dough until firm, about 30 minutes. Meanwhile, adjust an oven rack in the middle position and heat the oven to 375°.

Place the frozen tart shell on a baking sheet. Gently press a piece of aluminum foil that has been sprayed with vegetable oil against the dough and over the edges of the tart pan. Fill the shell with pie weights, we use uncooked rice, and bake until the top edge of the dough just starts to color and the surface of the dough under the foil no longer looks wet, about 30 minutes.

Remove the tart shell from the oven and carefully remove the foil and weights. Sprinkle the Parmesan evenly over the bottom of the tart shell, then return to the oven and continue to bake until the cheese is golden brown, 5-10 minutes. Set the pie shell aside to cool. Increase the oven temperature to 425°.

For the filling: Meanwhile, spread the zucchini and tomato out over several layers of paper towels. Sprinkle with 1/2 teaspoon salt and let drain for 30 minutes; gently blot the tops of the zucchini dry with paper towels before using. In a small bowl, whisk 2 tablespoons of the olive oil and the garlic together; set aside. In a separate bowl, mix the ricotta, Parmesan, and half the mozzarella together and season with salt and pepper to taste.

Spread the ricotta mixture evenly over the bottom of the cooled tart shell. Shingle the tomatoes on top of the ricotta and then shingle the zucchini attractively in concentric circles on top of the tomato, starting at the outside edge. Drizzle the garlic and olive oil mixture evenly over the zucchini. Bake the tart until the cheese is bubbling and the zucchini is slightly wilted, 20 minutes. Sprinkle remaining mozzarella over top and bake an additional 5 minutes until cheese is melted and golden brown.

Let the tart cool slightly on a wire rack for 5 minutes, then sprinkle with the basil. Remove the tart from the tart pan and transfer to a serving platter or cutting board. Cut into wedges and serve. The finished tart can also be held at room temperature for up to 1 hour before serving.

SIDES

All our main dishes come with one or two sides depending on the makeup of the meal. We carefully consider the composition of each plate and consequently need a variety of "go to" choices. The following recipes are our favorites.

THE
TRELLIS HOUSE

SIDES

Funeral Potatoes

Orange Glazed Sausages

Rosemary Home Fries with Roasted Tomato Aioli

Breakfast Potatoes With Peppers And Onions

Candy Bacon

Fruit Salad

Good Bacon and Breakfast Sausages

Funeral Potatoes

16 Servings

Ok, I know this recipe is not fancy, and it's not going to win any awards, but trust me when I say it DOES impress. You just gotta go for it sometimes! Alternatively, bring to a potluck or funeral and you will win friends and influence people. Ps. Whenever any guests ask for this recipe, which is every time we serve it, I cringe in horror and often lie about the cream of chicken soup part. Alas, my secret is out.

1 bag (8 cups) frozen shredded hash brown potatoes
3 tablespoons melted butter
1 small onion chopped fine
1 small can diced green chilies
1 can condensed cream of chicken soup
2 cups sharp cheddar cheese divided
1 pint sour cream
4 scallions sliced thinly
1 teaspoon ground black pepper
1 teaspoon garlic powder

Preheat oven to 400°. Mix all ingredients in a large bowl reserving 1 cup of cheese. Pour into buttered 9x13 inch baking dish and sprinkle with remaining cheese. Bake in middle of oven until golden and bubbly, about 45 minutes to an hour. Let cool for 30 minutes before serving. We let it cool to room temperature and then use an ice cream scoop and grill portions on a buttered skillet before serving. The hot, creamy potatoes with a crunchy griddled crust is impossible to resist.

Orange Glazed Sausages

16 sausages

16 good quality uncooked pork breakfast sausages
1 tablespoon orange marmalade
juice of one orange
1 tablespoon butter

Brown sausages in a large pan until cooked through. Add orange juice, butter, and marmalade to pan and simmer, shaking pan occasionally, until liquid is reduced and syrupy and sausages are glazed and fully coated. Serve warm.

Rosemary Home Fries with Roasted Tomato Aioli

8 Servings

Whenever we make our signature Eggs Benedict I always have a few roasted tomatoes leftover which I love to use for this sauce to add extra punch to these home fries. These potatoes are fragrant and crisp and addictive and made even more decadent by the aioli. This recipe comes from Bobby Flay.

Home Fries:
4 pounds russet potatoes
kosher salt and black pepper
1/4 cup canola oil
2 tablespoons fresh rosemary leaves
2 garlic cloves minced
1 slice good quality bacon, minced
1/4 cup parmesan
1/4 cup chopped parsley

Roasted Tomato Aioli:
1 plum tomato halved seeded and roasted
1/2 small onion chopped
2 garlic cloves chopped
1 teaspoon paprika
1 cup Hellman's mayonnaise
dash tabasco or other hot sauce

For the Aioli: Place all ingredients in a blender and process until smooth. Scrape into a small bowl, cover, and refrigerate for a few hours to let the flavors meld. Aioli can be made up to 24 hours in advance.

For the Home Fries: Put the potatoes in a pot and cover with water by 2 inches. Season the water with a teaspoon of salt. Bring to a boil and cook for about 20 minutes until the potatoes meet slight resistance when pierced with a skewer. Drain, cool enough to handle and cut into 1 inch dice.

Meanwhile combine the oil and rosemary in a blender, season with salt and pepper and blend for 1 minute. Let the oil sit for 30 minutes and then strain through a fine mesh strainer into a small bowl.

Heat the rosemary oil in a large skillet. Add the bacon and cook until golden and crisp. Remove and set aside. Add the potatoes, season with salt and pepper, and cook until golden brown and crusty on all sides, about 5 minutes. Add the garlic and cook for another 2 or 3 minutes and then stir in the bacon, Parmesan, and parsley.

Breakfast Potatoes With Peppers And Onions

8 Servings

Our guests love the surprise addition of sweet potatoes in our breakfast potatoes. We often make extra potatoes and then use them in frittatas the following morning.

5 pounds red bliss, Yukon gold, and sweet potatoes
  cut into spears or chunks
4 cloves garlic chopped fine
1 large white onion cut into 1 inch pieces
1 large green pepper seeded and cut into 1 inch pieces
1 large red pepper seeded and cut into 1 inch pieces
1/4 cup olive oil
1/2 stick butter cut into 4 pieces
2 teaspoons Lawry's seasoned salt
1 teaspoon cayenne
1 teaspoon fresh ground black pepper
1 teaspoon onion powder

Preheat the oven to 400°. Place the potatoes on a large rimmed baking sheet. Add remaining ingredients and mix with your hands until seasonings are well distributed. Bake for 40-45 minutes, shaking the pan and stirring the potatoes a few times with a spatula. Raise the heat to 450° and bake until crisp and brown, flipping one additional time for 15-20 minutes more. Taste and add a bit more seasoned salt before serving if needed.

Candy Bacon

12 Servings

Whenever we have bacon on our menu board I always write "Good" Bacon! It's hard to improve upon good bacon but this recipe does the trick.

24 slices good quality thick cut bacon
1 tablespoon Dijon mustard
1/2 cup maple syrup
2 tablespoons brown sugar
black pepper

Preheat oven to 400°. Place two wire racks in two baking sheets and spray with vegetable oil. Lay bacon slices side by side on each rack. Stir together mustard and syrup vigorously with a fork and then brush lightly on each slice of bacon. Sprinkle with brown sugar and season with black pepper. Bake for 20 minutes, monitoring bacon regularly to make sure it is cooking evenly and doesn't burn. Cook a bit longer until bacon is brown and crisp. Remove from oven and loosen bacon from racks using tongs or slices will stick.

Fruit Salad

8 Servings

Fruit salad is always a welcomed side dish. We try to keep it very simple. Any fruit that goes well together will do.

1 bunch green seedless grapes halved
1 pint ripe strawberries hulled and halved
1 pint blueberries washed and picked over
1 pint raspberries or blackberries
1/2 cantaloupe or honeydew melon seeded and
    cut into large dice
3 Kiwis peeled and sliced
2 oranges peeled and cut into segments
mint sprigs

Mix all fruit in a bowl and squeeze a few orange segments on top. Serve in individual bowls and garnish with mint sprig.

Good Bacon and Breakfast Sausages

Ha! There is no recipe here as you can see. The point is folks, buy the very best thick cut, smoked bacon that you can find. Same with breakfast sausage. Moving on...

TURNDOWN
FAVORITES

I knew even before we opened our doors that I wanted to leave a sweet treat for each guest before bedtime.
I knew that nothing would be appreciated more than coming home to a freshly spruced up room and a fresh baked good with a handpicked bouquet of flowers from our garden.
The challenge is baking the right treats.

THE
TRELLIS HOUSE

TURNDOWN FAVORITES

Trellis House Lemon Cake

Jam Oaties

Thumbprint Coconut Cookies

Trellis House Blondies

Best Lemon Squares

Apricot Walnut Rugelach

Chocolate Chip and Nut Brownies

Maine Farmer Cookies

Pecan Pie Bars

Trellis House Lemon Cake

8 Servings

Whenever we learn one of our guests is celebrating a special occasion we sneak into their room while they are at dinner and leave this very special cake and a fresh bouquet of flowers. There is no lemon in the cake but it is soaked in lemon syrup while still warm and is perfect day or night.

1 cup butter softened
1 cup sugar
2 large eggs
1 1/2 cups flour sifted
1/2 teaspoon salt
1 teaspoon baking powder
1/2 cup whole milk or buttermilk

Syrup:
1/3 cup sugar
juice of 1 lemon
zest of half a lemon

Glaze:
1 cup confectioners' sugar
2 tablespoons lemon juice

Preheat oven to 350°. Butter two 6 inch cake loaf pans and line with buttered parchment paper. Cream 1 cup butter and 1 cup sugar together. Add eggs, one at a time, beating well until mixture is light and fluffy. Sift flour with salt and baking powder, add to first mixture, alternately with milk, beating well. Pour batter into pans and bake about 40 minutes until tester comes out clean or with moist crumbs attached.

For the lemon syrup: Mix 1/3 cup sugar with lemon juice and zest in a small saucepan, heat until sugar is dissolved and pour over cake in pan while cake is still warm. Let cool to room temperature before removing cake from pan.

For the lemon glaze: Stir 1 cup confectioners' sugar and 2 tablespoons lemon juice together until smooth. Pour over cooled cake and spread to an even layer.

"Weekend Getaway!"

Everything was perfect. The details such as a homemade delicious brownie - all well thought out. Breakfast was devine and even included the Trellis House mimosa!!! Service was warm and fun! The location of course is perfect...just a short walk to great restaurants and beaches.

Jam Oaties

16 Bars

This is the perfect late night treat. Just a few ingredients come together in an old fashioned, sweet, salty, and fruity delicacy which we cut into bars for a late night bite.

1 3/4 sticks salted butter cut into pieces
1 1/2 cups flour
1 1/2 cups old fashioned rolled oats
1 cup packed brown sugar
1 teaspoon baking powder
1/2 teaspoon salt
10-12 ounces strawberry or any jam of choice

Preheat the oven to 350°. Butter a 9-inch square baking pan. In an electric stand mixer beat together the butter, flour, oats, brown sugar, baking powder and salt until the consistency of coarse meal. Press half the oat mixture into the prepared pan. Spread with the strawberry preserves. Sprinkle the other half of the oat mixture evenly over the top and pat lightly. Bake until light brown, 30-40 minutes. Let cool completely and then cut into squares.

Thumbprint Coconut Cookies

32 Cookies

I have been making these melt in your mouth cookies for as long as I can remember. The addition of the coconut makes them otherworldly. Trust me, these cookies are worth the effort. They are actually very easy but take some patience.

3 sticks unsalted butter room temperature
1 cup sugar
1 teaspoon vanilla
3 1/2 cups flour
1/4 teaspoon salt
1 large egg beaten with 1 tablespoon water
7 ounces sweetened shredded coconut
raspberry and/or apricot jam

Preheat oven to 350°. In an electric stand mixer fitted with a paddle attachment, cream together the butter and sugar until just combined and then add the vanilla. Separately, sift together the flour and salt. With the mixer on low speed, add the flour mixture. Mix until the dough starts to come together. Turn onto a floured board and roll into a flat disc, wrap in plastic wrap and chill for 30 minutes.

Roll the dough into 1 1/4 inch balls. Dip each ball into egg wash and then roll in coconut. Place the balls on an ungreased cookie sheet and press a slight indentation into the top with your thumb or finger. Drop1/4 teaspoon of jam into each indentation. Bake for 20-25 minutes, until the coconut is a golden brown. Cool on baking sheet for a few minutes and then remove to wire rack.

TRELLIS HOUSE BLONDIES

16 Bars

Have you ever had a Blondie and not wished it was a brownie? Well now is your chance to make that right. This Blondie is utterly amazing. Butterscotch notes with an ideal balance of chocolate and nuts. Everyone loves this little snack before bed!

1 cup pecans or walnuts toasted and chopped
1 1/2 cups flour
1 teaspoon baking powder
1/2 teaspoon salt
12 tablespoons butter melted and cooled
1 1/2 cups light brown sugar packed
2 large eggs lightly beaten
2 teaspoons vanilla extract

1 cup pecans or walnuts chopped
1/2 cup white chocolate chips
1/2 cups semi-sweet chocolate chips

Heat oven to 350° and spray a 9-inch square baking pan
with vegetable spray. Whisk flour, baking powder, and salt
together in medium bowl. In another bowl, use a rubber
spatula to combine the melted butter and brown sugar.
Stir in eggs and vanilla and mix well. Fold in dry ingredients
until just combined. Fold in chocolate and nuts and pour
batter into prepared pan, smoothing top with rubber
spatula. Bake until top is shiny, cracked, and light golden
brown, 22-25 minutes; do not overbake. Cool on wire rack
to room temperature. Cut into 2-inch squares and serve.

Best Lemon Squares

16 Squares

When I was a boy, *The Peanut's Cookbook* was my baking bible. My very favorite recipe was Lucy's lemon squares. Linus's Linzer cookies were a close second. I have always held Lucy's lemon squares up as the highest of benchmarks. These lemon squares cannot be beat. Everyone loves them and asks for the recipe. The crust is buttery and crunchy and the filling is a wonderful texture, not too tart and not too sweet.

Crust:
1/2-pound (2 sticks) unsalted butter room temperature
1/2 cup granulated sugar
2 cups all-purpose flour
1/8 teaspoon kosher salt
2 teaspoons grated lemon zest

Filling:
6 large eggs room temperature
3 cups granulated sugar
2 tablespoons grated lemon zest
1 cup freshly squeezed lemon juice
1 cup all-purpose flour sifted
confectioners' sugar for dusting

Preheat the oven to 350° and spray a 9X13 inch pan with vegetable spray.

For the crust: Cream the butter and sugar in an electric stand mixer fitted with the paddle attachment until light. Combine the flour, salt and 2 teaspoons lemon zest with the butter mixture and mix on low until just combined. Turn the dough into the prepared pan and press evenly and firmly into the bottom of the pan. Bake in the lower third of the oven for 15 minutes, until golden to just light brown.

Meanwhile, whisk the eggs, sugar, 2 tablespoons lemon zest, lemon juice and flour. Pour over the crust and continue baking for 30 minutes or so until the filling is set. It will brown in some areas but that's ok. You must let this completely cool to room temperature or the filling will be a bit gooey and won't cut cleanly. Once cool cut into squares and then sift confectioners' sugar over top. We serve these squares in little paper cupcake liners. We think they are even better the next day.

Apricot Walnut Rugelach

48 Cookies

I grew up eating rugelach. The flaky cream cheese dough loaded with cinnamon, sugar, and raisins is my personal ultimate favorite cookie. I buy them every time I go to a Jewish deli or bakery. We often serve them in a cookie jar in the afternoons.

8 ounces cream cheese room temperature
1/2 pound unsalted butter room temperature
1/4 cup sugar plus 9 tablespoons
1/4 teaspoon Kosher salt
1 teaspoon vanilla extract
2 cups all-purpose flour
1/4 cup light brown sugar packed
1 1/2 teaspoons ground cinnamon
3/4 cup raisins
1 cup walnuts finely chopped
1/2 cup apricot preserves pureed in a food processor
1 egg beaten with 1 tablespoon of milk

Cream the cheese and the butter in a bowl with an electric mixer until light. Add 1/4 cup granulated sugar, the salt, and vanilla. With the mixer on low speed, add the flour and mix just until combined. Place the dough onto a well-floured board and roll into a ball. Cut the ball in quarters, shape into disks, wrap each piece in plastic, and refrigerate for 1 hour.

For the Filling: Combine 6 tablespoons of the sugar, the brown sugar, 1/2 teaspoon cinnamon, the raisins, and walnuts.

On a well-floured board, roll each ball of dough into one 9-inch circle. Spread the dough with 2 tablespoons of the apricot preserves and sprinkle with 1/2 cup of the filling. Press the filling down lightly into the dough. Cut the circles into 12 equal wedges, (I use a pizza wheel), cutting the circle in quarters, then each quarter into thirds. Starting with the wide edge, roll up each wedge. Place the cookies, points tucked under, on a baking sheet lined with parchment paper. Chill for 30 minutes.

Preheat oven to 350°. Brush each cookie with the egg wash. Combine remaining 3 tablespoons sugar and 1 teaspoon cinnamon and sprinkle on the cookies. Bake for 18-20 minutes, until lightly browned. Remove to a wire rack and let cool.

Chocolate Chip and Nut Brownies

12 Bars

This is a variation of the classic recipe shared by Katherine Hepburn. Much like its author (Hepburn not Plotkin), this recipe is a no-fuss classic. It helps greatly if while making this recipe you suck in your cheeks and bark annoying comments at people passing through the kitchen in a warbly, superior voice.

1/2 cup best quality cocoa
1/2 cup butter (1 stick)
2 eggs
1 cup sugar
1/4 cup flour
1 cup chopped walnuts or pecans lightly toasted in a pan
3/4 cup semi-sweet chocolate morsels
1 teaspoon vanilla
pinch of salt

Heat oven to 325°. Melt butter in saucepan with cocoa and stir until smooth. Remove from heat and allow to cool. Transfer to a large bowl. Whisk in eggs, one at a time, beating vigorously between each addition. Stir in vanilla.

In a separate bowl, combine sugar, flour, nuts, chocolate, and salt. Add to the cocoa-butter mixture. Stir until just combined.

Pour into an 8 x 8-inch-square pan sprayed with vegetable oil. Bake 30 to 35 minutes. Do not overbake; the brownies should be gooey. Let cool, then cut into bars.

"Paramount Experience"

Common Space, Grounds, and Room Accommodations all finely appointed with nothing left to be desired. It is clear that the owners have poured there heart and soul into every detail to ensure guests have a special experience. BREAKFAST...WOW....Don't you dare sleep in!!! Truly the best breakfast meals we have experienced in all our travels. We look forward to many returns.

Maine Farmer Cookies

20 Cookies

You may know this recipe as Cowboy cookies but when in Maine...

1 1/4 cups all-purpose flour
3/4 teaspoon baking powder
1/2 teaspoon baking soda
1/2 teaspoon salt
1 1/2 cups packed light brown sugar
12 tablespoons unsalted butter melted and cooled
1 large egg plus 1 large yolk
1 teaspoon vanilla extract
1 1/4 cups old fashioned rolled oats
1 cup pecans toasted and chopped coarse
1 cup shredded coconut
2/3 cup semisweet chocolate chips

Adjust oven rack to middle position and heat oven to 350°. Line 2 rimless cookie sheets with parchment paper. Whisk flour, baking powder, baking soda, and salt together in bowl.

Whisk sugar, melted butter, egg and yolk, and vanilla in large bowl until combined. Stir in flour mixture until no dry streaks remain. Stir in oats, pecans, coconut, and chocolate chips until fully combined (mixture will be sticky).

Lightly spray 1/4-cup dry measuring cup with vegetable oil . Drop level 1/4-cup portions of dough onto prepared sheets, staggering 8 portions per sheet and spacing them about 2 1/2 inches apart. Divide any remaining dough among portions.

Bake cookies, 1 sheet at a time, until edges are browned and set and centers are puffed with pale, raw spots, 15 to 17 minutes, rotating sheet halfway through baking. Do not overbake.

Let cookies cool on sheet for 5 minutes, then transfer to wire rack and let cool completely before serving. Cookies can be stored in airtight container for up to 3 days.

Pecan Pie Bars

16 Bars

Crust:
1 cup unbleached all-purpose flour
1/3 cup packed light brown sugar
1/4 cup toasted pecans chopped coarse
1/4 teaspoon baking powder
6 tablespoons cold butter cut into pieces

Pecan Filling:
1/2 cup packed light brown sugar
1/3 cup light corn syrup
4 tablespoons unsalted butter (½ stick), melted
1 tablespoon bourbon or dark rum
2 teaspoons vanilla extract
1/2 teaspoon table salt
1 large egg lightly beaten
2 cups toasted pecans chopped coarse

Toast all of the pecans for the recipe (2 ¼ cups) on a rimmed baking sheet in a 350° oven until fragrant, about 8 minutes, stirring once.

For the crust: Adjust oven rack to middle position and heat oven to 350°. Spray a 9 inch square baking pan with nonstick cooking spray. Fold two 16 inch pieces of foil or parchment paper lengthwise to measure 9 inches wide.

Fit one sheet in bottom of buttered pan, pushing it into corners and up sides of pan (overhang will help in removal of baked bars). Fit second sheet in pan in same manner, perpendicular to first sheet. Spray sheets with nonstick cooking spray.

Place flour, brown sugar, 1 cup toasted pecans, salt and baking powder in food processor. Process mixture until it resembles coarse cornmeal, about five 1 second pulses. Add butter and pulse until mixture resembles sand, about eight 1 second pulses. Pat mixture evenly into prepared pan and bake until crust is light brown and springs back when touched, about 20 minutes.

For the pecan filling: While crust bakes, whisk together brown sugar, melted butter, corn syrup, bourbon, vanilla, and salt in medium bowl until just combined. Add egg and whisk until incorporated. Pour filling on top of hot crust and sprinkle 1/4 cup pecans evenly over top. Bake until top is brown and cracks start to form across surface, 22-25 minutes. Cool on wire rack for 1 hour.

Remove bars from pan using foil or parchment handles and transfer to cutting board. Cut into bars.

COOKING
SCHOOL

The Trellis House

loves food and cooking!

We offer cooking classes to groups

of 6 to 8 guests which culminates

with a lovely dinner party

at the end of the class.

This is a great way to make new friends,

learn how to stuff a lobster

and of course have one of the

best meals of your life, guaranteed.

THE
TRELLIS HOUSE
—:—

COOKING SCHOOL

Glen's Cole Slaw

Grilled Mustard Shrimp with Pineapple Salsa

Trellis House Seafood Baked Stuffed Lobsters

Twice Baked Scallion and Cheddar Potatoes

Blueberry or Raspberry Cobbler

Glen's Cole Slaw

8 Servings

We are very discerning when it comes to a delicious, old-school coleslaw. This simple recipe never disappoints.

8 cups cabbage shredded or chopped
1/2 cup carrots shredded
1 1/3 cups Hellman's mayonnaise
3 tablespoons white vinegar
2 tablespoons sugar
2 tablespoons milk
2 teaspoons dried minced onion
salt and pepper

Combine all ingredients except cabbage and carrots in a large bowl and whisk until smooth. Add cabbage and carrots and toss well. Cover and chill in the refrigerator several hours before serving. Season to taste.

Grilled Mustard Shrimp with Pineapple Salsa

40 Pieces

This recipe makes the most flavorful, delicious and special shrimp you can imagine. During our most recent class one of my guests exclaimed "these are the best shrimp I have ever eaten"! There is no better compliment.

Mustard Marinade:
2 cloves garlic finely minced
1 sweet onion finely minced
1/4 cup fresh parsley minced
1/4 cup fresh basil minced
1 teaspoon dry mustard
2 teaspoons Dijon mustard
2 tablespoons kosher salt
1/4 teaspoon freshly ground black pepper
1/4 cup olive oil
juice zest and juice of 1 lemon
40 jumbo shrimp, tails on deveined and peeled
wooden skewers

Pineapple Salsa:
2 tablespoons olive oil
1 1/2 cups minced sweet onion
2 teaspoons fresh ginger grated

1 1/2 teaspoons garlic finely minced

1/2 ripe pineapple peeled seeded & small diced

1/3 cup freshly squeezed orange juice

2 teaspoons light brown sugar

1 teaspoon kosher salt

1/2 teaspoon fresh ground black pepper

1 small jalapeño pepper seeded and minced

2 teaspoons fresh mint very finely chopped

For the marinade: Combine the garlic, onion, parsley, basil, mustards, salt, pepper, olive oil, and lemon juice. Add the shrimp and allow them to marinate for 1 hour at room temperature or cover and refrigerate for up to 2 days. Prepare a gas or charcoal grill. Place 5 or 6 shrimp on each 12 inch skewer. Grill each skewer for about 2 minutes on each side.

For the pineapple salsa: Sauté the oil, onions, and ginger in a large sauté pan over medium-low heat for 10 minutes, or until the onions are translucent. Add the garlic and cook for 1 minute more. Add the mango, reduce heat to low and cook for 10 minutes more. Add the orange juice, brown sugar, salt, pepper, and jalapenos. Cook for 10 more minutes, or until orange juice is reduced, stirring occasionally. Remove from the heat and add the mint. Transfer to a bowl and serve at room temperature or chilled with shrimp.

Trellis House
Seafood Stuffing

8 Servings

When we go out for lobster dinner my favorite thing to order is a baked, stuffed, one and half pound lobster, and being me, I am never completely satisfied with the stuffing. Here is my own ideal version of what stuffing for seafood should be.

4 sleeves Ritz crackers
1 stick butter
1 small onion finely chopped
2 celery stalks finely chopped
3/4 to 1 pound peeled and deveined Maine shrimp, whole or roughly chopped
3/4 to 1 pound sea scallops whole or roughly chopped depending on size
3/4 to 1 pound haddock filet
salt and freshly ground black pepper
2 teaspoons Worcestershire
1 teaspoon dry mustard
2 tablespoons Hellman's mayonnaise
1/4 cup minced fresh parsley
paprika

Roughly crush Ritz crackers into a large bowl. Heat 1/2 stick of butter in a large sauté pan and add onions and celery. Cook until translucent and softened. Pour over Ritz crackers. Melt remaining butter in hot pan and add shrimp, scallops and haddock. Cook, stirring intermittently, until seafood is just cooked through. Break Haddock into small pieces and flake which also indicates it is done.

Pour seafood mixture and a majority of the liquid (reserving some as needed) over cracker mixture, add Worcestershire, mustard, mayonnaise and parsley and gently stir until combined. Stuffing should be moist and just hold its shape. Season with salt and pepper and add water or reserved seafood liquid if more moisture is needed. Use stuffing in lobster, fish or baked stuffed shrimp. After stuffing seafood, dot with butter and dust with paprika.

Trellis House Seafood Baked Stuffed Lobsters

Serves 8

There is nothing better than everyone having their own gorgeous baked stuffed lobster to feast on. This is our version and we think it doesn't get better! Warning: you must be ok with murderous actions and a meaningful amount of blood and guts to follow this recipe. Now, no one feels good about this sort of activity but If the idea doesn't sound possible for you please read no further. Just turn the page and order a pizza.

8 - 1 1/4 or larger sized live lobsters

1 recipe Trellis House Seafood Stuffing (see page 208)

2 large rimmed baking sheets
1 stick of softened butter for dotting lobsters
4 lemons sliced very thin

Preheat oven to 425°.

Place a lobster on its back. Using a very heavy knife or cleaver plunge the tip of the knife into the victim just below its mandible (mouth parts) and using a sawing motion continue down the body until you reach the end of the tail. Do not cut all the way through to the cutting board. The idea is to be able to split the lobster apart. Now, spread the lobster apart with your hands and a kitchen rag, cracking some shell to allow space for the following action: reach into the poor creature's middles and remove any innards such as the intestines, etc. I remove any roe but that's your decision.

Ok, relax, the ugliness is over....for now.

Take your glorious stuffing and gently mound inside and top of the cavity you just created. Stuffing should extend the entire length of the lobster. Place on a baking sheet stuffing side up.

Now repeat 7 more times.

Dot each stuffing mound/lobster generously with butter. Layer on lemon slices decoratively on each and sprinkle with Paprika. Bake for about 20 minutes until lemons and stuffing are golden brown and lobster is bright red/orange. Place under broiler for a minute or two if your want a crispy top on your stuffing as I do. Enjoy! Serve with ramekins of melted butter.

Twice Baked Scallion and Cheddar Potatoes

10 Servings

Every barbecue must include twice baked potatoes in my opinion. I love the top crust when broiled to a delicious crunch.

5 russet potatoes scrubbed and dried
olive oil
Lawry's seasoned salt
4 tablespoons butter
2 tablespoons onion minced
1/4 cup buttermilk or whole milk
3/4 cup sour cream
4 green onions (white and green parts) sliced thinly
1 cup or more cheddar shredded or cut into small cubes
1/2 teaspoon salt
1/2 teaspoon freshly ground black pepper
paprika for sprinkling on top

Preheat oven to 400°. Wash and dry potatoes. Rub with olive oil and sprinkle with seasoned salt. Place potatoes on a baking sheet and bake for about 1 hour, turning over halfway through, until skins are very crisp and flesh is tender when pierced with a sharp knife. Remove from oven and let cool for about 15 minutes or until able to handle. Turn oven down to 350°.

Cut potatoes in half lengthwise. Scoop out flesh into a large bowl, leaving a thin layer of potato on the inside, to make 10 potato boats. Mash/whip potatoes with a fork, until smooth. Heat milk in microwave until hot. Stir milk into potatoes along with butter, onion, sour cream, and green onions, and mix well. Stir in cheese and season with salt and pepper. Spoon potato mixture into potato boats evenly, mounding in center; sprinkle lightly with paprika.

Place back in oven for about 20 minutes. Turn on broiler and bake until golden browned on top, about 5 minutes.

"Second time to this wonderful place"

We visited the Trellis house for our second time in September and we had a wonderful time. Laurence and Glen are two of the nicest people we've ever met; wonderful hosts that know how to make you feel right at home. We've met so many nice people during our stays, we can't wait to go back again soon. Everything about our stay was exceptional, from the delicious breakfasts to the beautiful location, it's a must-stay when visiting Ogunquit.

Blueberry or Raspberry Cobbler

8 Servings

This is a wonderful summer dessert and you can substitute any fruit you like. My favorites are blueberries, pears, and raspberries. Serve with vanilla ice cream for a crispy, buttery, fruity dessert.

1 stick butter melted
2 cups plus 2 tablespoons sugar
2 cups flour
2 heaping teaspoons baking powder
2 cups whole milk
2 pints blueberries or raspberries

Preheat the oven to 350°. Butter or spray with vegetable oil a large baking dish. In a medium bowl, whisk two cups sugar with the flour, baking powder and milk. Whisk in the melted butter. Rinse the berries and pat them dry. Pour the batter into the baking dish. Sprinkle the berries evenly over the top of the batter and then sprinkle reserved sugar over the top. Bake until golden brown and bubbly, about 1 hour.

CPSIA information can be obtained
at www.ICGtesting.com
Printed in the USA
BVHW022318030222
627406BV00001B/1